W9-BEH-506

# Making Ethical Decisions

# Making Ethical Decisions

*A Casebook*

# Louis B. Weeks

**The Westminster Press**
Philadelphia

© 1987 Louis B. Weeks

*All rights reserved*—no part of this book may be reproduced in any form without permission in writing from the publisher, except by a reviewer who wishes to quote brief passages in connection with a review in magazine or newspaper.

Scripture quotations from the Revised Standard Version of the Bible are copyrighted 1946, 1952, © 1971, 1973 by the Division of Christian Education of the National Council of the Churches of Christ in the U.S.A. and are used by permission.

Grateful acknowledgment is made to the Case Study Institute for permission to reprint the following copyrighted material: "Clark Roberts and the 'Previous Life' Reading" and "Planning Monday," copyright © 1977; "Deadline March 14," copyright © 1978; and "Global Village Living," copyright © 1979.

Book design by Gene Harris

First edition

Published by The Westminster Press®
Philadelphia, Pennsylvania

PRINTED IN THE UNITED STATES OF AMERICA

9  8  7  6  5  4  3  2  1

Library of Congress Cataloging-in-Publication Data

Weeks, Louis, 1941–
    Making ethical decisions.

    Bibliography: p.
    1. Christian ethics—Decision making—Case
studies. 2. Decision-making (Ethics)—Case studies.
I. Title.
BJ1251.W44  1987      241      87–14703
ISBN 0-664-24064-X (pbk.)

# Contents

Preface and Acknowledgments     7

Introduction
Branford Shanty     11

PART ONE: Questions About Christian Living

1 What Shall I Do?     21
    What Is an Ethical Decision?   23
    A Look at History   25
    Christian Principles and Human Situations   27

2 How Do I Choose?     30
    Community and Commitment   32
    Character and Ethics   34
    What Is a Case?   36

3 How Shall I Live?     39
    Am I a Saint?   41
    Am I a Disciple?   42
    Am I a Pilgrim?   44
    Am I Telling a Story?   45
    Am I Born Again?   47

4 How Shall I Grow?     48
    Do We Develop in Stages?   50
    Do Adults Move Through "Moral Stages"?   51
    Does Gender Make a Difference?   53
    What About "Stages in Life"?   54
    Other Factors in Decision Making   55

**PART TWO: The Cases**

5 Decisions in Personal and Family Life                     59
   "This House Is a Mess!"   59
   Second Home   63
   Global-Village Living   67
   Clark Roberts and the Previous-Life Reading   71

6 Decisions in Ministry                                      76
   The Death of Fanny Grimes   76
   Easter Sunrise   80
   The *Psychology Today* Questionnaire   88
   Deadline: March 14   93

7 Decisions in Vocation and Political Life                   98
   Bradley Johnson, Volunteer   98
   "You Get Back What You Sow"   102
   Planning Monday   105
   Expense Account Blues   114

Further Reading                                             117

# Preface and Acknowledgments

This is a study book for Christians. I wrote it to evoke thought and discussion in small groups, church school classes, and families. Along the way, may it also provide some insights and offer encouragement for Christians in living, for individuals can read it and learn something too. But first it should serve people learning from one another and from the Bible, as well as from other resources for Christians today.

Though sorely tempted at times, I refrained from writing an ethics textbook. Instead, this effort consists of a baker's dozen of case studies, along with succinct notes to aid in discussing those situations. Some of the cases are complex, involving many people and controversial issues, challenging ordinary Christians in new areas of ethical consideration. Other cases are personal, seemingly simple, and require concentration on familiar values and commitments already prized. In every case, people who seek to be faithful encounter some decision—frequently a number of decisions.

Along with the cases and discussion notes, I ask questions about Christian ethics and explore very briefly some areas in which ethicists are working. Their insights and illustrations seem pertinent for us all. Space limitations mean I can only invite readers to ask those questions and introduce those areas of work. Suggestions for further reading (at the back of the book) may help readers pursue additional study.

When representatives of the Men's Program of the Presbyterian Church (U.S.A.) asked me to offer a casebook, I jumped at the chance. Many men in churches today can benefit from study together, just as women do. Though the pressures on male members of Western societies seem somewhat different from those on female members, identifiable needs are present. For almost all, study and fellowship together can contribute to growth.

I give thanks to God daily that we live in an era when women share increasingly in all kinds of Christian ministry. My prayers continue that the time will soon come when full partnership among Christians of both sexes will be the ordinary expectation in all communions.

The intention to write for study groups comprised of men influenced my choice of cases and notes. For some years I wrote and preached unconscious of the sexism in my language and in my choice of illustration. Characteristic of unthinking men, I also frequently used examples of sick women and healthy men. Some of my early sermons and articles make me cringe, as I cringe when men or women use such loaded examples today.

In this book, most of the cases and illustrations involve males just as most materials written for women use illustrations of females. Nevertheless, some cases represent the perspective of women, and at least one case purposely does not give the gender of the major character. Perhaps some of the discussions generated by the cases, like some of the teachings about ethics, will involve both men and women in the issues related to gender today.

A few words about the way the book proceeds. Case study almost has to start with a case. Mine is a complicated one, Branford Shanty, about an issue facing Christians right now: How do we in the United States respond to the situation in the Republic of South Africa? The issue is related to many others, as the text shows. The major character may be responding to the issues in a way different from most of us. However, we can all learn of ways to witness from the attempts of other Christians to live their faith. A discussion note accompanies this first case, and similar notes appear with the remainder of the cases.

After Branford Shanty comes Part One, four chapters that ask questions about Christian living. In each chapter, my own thinking and that of others serve as guides for your discussions. I relate the Branford Shanty case to each question and to some of the reflections in those chapters. You may use this example as you study the other cases.

The four questions are simple enough on the surface: "What shall I do?" "How do I choose?" "How shall I live?" "How do I grow?" The first enables us to remember the nature of the Christian gospel as we look at ethics. The second opens exploration of the nature of Christian character and community, as well as providing a word about case study among believers. The third question evokes some images of the Christian life that have been used by believers in thinking about moral issues. And the fourth elicits findings from ethicists about people today, discoveries that are affecting religious education and church life considerably.

You may find some questions more intriguing than others. You are welcome to pass by those you find less helpful. In a way, all these discursive chapters serve as a preface for Part Two, the actual cases themselves.

These cases are offered in gradually widening areas. Four personal and familial cases are followed by four that are related to congregational decisions, and the last four involve community and vocational decisions. They were all prepared as a basis for discussion, rather than to illustrate either effective or ineffective handling of a situation. Names, dates, and places have been changed, but the events occurred essentially as reported.

In discussing these cases, I sincerely invite men and women to talk about their own work and witness in constructive ways. Frequently in congregations we seem to hide our attempts to live in Christian discipleship, we belittle or ignore the struggles of others, and we wonder why church seems irrelevant to the workaday world. It does not have to be that way. When we feel free to share something of our efforts and worries about issues and problems we face, we gather strength for living, joy, and a sense of solidarity with other Christians. The Holy Spirit dwells in the relationships among Christians, and God rejoices when we bear one another's burden, fulfilling the law of Christ.

A number of friends and colleagues helped in this effort. I am particularly grateful to those who provided information and perspective for the cases, even though I cannot name them. Those people remained patient and helpful through a process of interviewing and proofreading that at times became tedious. Their actual experiences form the substance of this book.

David Lewis of the Men's Program of the Presbyterian Church (U.S.A.) not only initiated this project but also offered suggestions for improving the discursive chapters. Several colleagues on the faculty of Louisville Presbyterian Theological Seminary read all or parts of the typescript, and I appreciate their advice and encouragement. Hal Warheim, John Mulder, David Hester, and Nancy Ramsay lent special talents and energies, and I tried to follow their advice where I could.

Over the past eight years, study groups in Louisville at Anchorage, Briargate, Calvin, Fourth, Grace Hope, Iroquois, Second, and several other Presbyterian churches have from time to time engaged in case study, and I have learned from their examples about good adult Christian education. I tried to keep their interests in mind as I selected cases and wrote notes for them. Many of these cases were first discussed among those groups.

I am indebted also to colleagues who have helped me learn about cases. Friends from business schools, from other seminaries, and from a number of colleges have actively exchanged materials and ideas with me for more than a decade. Members of the Association for Case Teaching have been most active in that process; to them, many thanks.

"Global-Village Living" was written for presentation as a portion of the 1979 T. V. Moore Lectures at San Francisco Theological Seminary. The author expresses appreciation to those responsible for the event.

The typescript received careful attention from Norma Porterfield, who helps in so many other areas of ministry as well. And, again, members of the Weeks family contributed greatly, sharing experiences and reading diligently the various drafts.

The writing, choice of cases, explanations of ideas, and possible errors remain my responsibility. I hope they do not interfere with your learning.

L.W.

# Introduction

## BRANFORD SHANTY

Tom White sat with twenty-nine others on the porch of the administration building, under the sign that said BURSAR. He felt uncomfortable and out of place amid the undergraduates around him. Members of the group, surrounded by other students and police in the yard and on the Branford sidewalks, were preparing to move to the other door, the one that said TREASURER OF THE UNIVERSITY. To do so would mean arrest and perhaps expulsion from school.

Tom wished that Jenny, his wife, could be here to help him decide what to do. As a second-year law student he faced exams early next week—fully a week earlier than the undergraduates. He did consider apartheid worth combating. He wished Branford University would divest its holdings in companies with major investments in South Africa. But was this action correct for him? Doubts erupted. His family commitments? His commitment to law? Would arrest jeopardize his chance to practice? Would expulsion cost him the law review position? What should he do?

After an undergraduate program focused on political science and history, Tom White, 24, had moved naturally to the law school at Branford University. He and Jenny were married as both graduated from college. Jenny's major had been elementary education and mathematics, and the Branford area offered good opportunities for her to find a teaching job.

Jenny and Tom White entered into the life of the community, joined the Third Presbyterian Church not far from campus, and registered to vote. They did not consider themselves particularly "righteous" or "Christian" in their activities or worldviews. They did sense God's presence in the world, and they considered Jesus Christ savior. They believed God cared for the whole world, and they considered all peoples tied together by God's Spirit and by the stewardship of natural resources given in creation.

They also tried to help others as one aspect of their religious commitment. During his first year of law school at Branford, Tom had donated five hours a week (all he could afford) to the community law center downtown. There he worked with other students and some members of the faculty and the local bar association to provide services for a limited number of poor people in the metropolitan area. Jenny stayed after school once a week to tutor children who had special needs.

At Third Presbyterian, the Whites tried to attend church school as well as worship. Their packed lives left little time for other activities, but they made it to an occasional family night dinner.

At one church dinner, in May, Jenny and Tom White heard a speaker from Soweto, a black township in the Johannesburg area of South Africa. He spoke of the effects of apartheid on the black majority in the nation, on the ways the National Party sought to govern by dividing tribes, and on the religious life of South African Christians, white and black. Afterward Jenny remarked to Tom on the gravity of the situation, and both she and he began to read even more about the peoples and politics of the southern African countries.

At a bookstore Jenny found *South Africa: Time Running Out,* a report of the Study Commission on U.S. Policy Toward Southern Africa (Berkeley, Cal.: University of California Press, 1981). This book not only contained a reasoned statement concerning policy for the United States regarding the Republic of South Africa, it also gave the Whites good information about the history and demographics of the nation and its neighbors.

At the law school Tom found whole sheafs of reports on South Africa and the responses of American-based transnationals and nonprofit institutions to movements for divestment. He also read pamphlets expounding the legal aspects of divestment. Some said such actions violated the requirement that trustees of money exercise prudent management of resources. Others showed that divestment did not necessarily lower returns. Still other reports found the South African economy to be risky or urged prudent investors to cease involvement for economic reasons alone.

In October Tom and Jenny heard another speaker at Third Presbyterian, a minister in the Evangelical Church of Lesotho, who preached on Micah. "Yes," he admitted, "the Basotho and the people of other tribes would suffer if jobs disappeared as transnationals withdrew. But only a minority of us are in monied industrial economies anyway." He also pointed out something that the Whites had not realized: citizens of South Africa or its so-called "homelands" could be arrested for treason if they advocated economic boycotts or disinvestment. Hence, Allan Boesak, Desmond Tutu, and other such recognized leaders were careful about what they said, even outside of their country. If they said more in support of divestment or boycotts, they would not be allowed to return home to continue the struggle for majority rights.

In December the Whites received at church school a copy of the statement to the 1985 General Assembly of the Presbyterian Church (U.S.A.) supporting a policy of selective divestment. The statement spoke of apartheid as a "heresy" because of the complicity of all in racial injustice. "The Presbyterian commitment to work within unjust structures for change does not require the church to ignore brick walls when it hits them," the report declared. "The Reformed commitment to engagement does not require continued adherence to a particular strategy or location; withdrawal from the corporation is hardly withdrawal from the world." The report stated plainly that divestment would not bring "purity." "All institutions are flawed by sin, corporations and churches included"—to which Tom and Jenny both said "Amen."

In January Tom attended a public forum on the question of divestment, sponsored by a newly formed Branford Coalition Against Apartheid. He heard university spokespersons express ignorance of the Sullivan Principles, for several years the standard of progressive involvement of American-based multinationals doing business in South Africa. A spokesperson promised that the board would certainly study those principles and doubtless would support shareholder initiatives to urge companies to sign them and abide by them.

The student-faculty coalition, which sought to involve townspeople as well, gathered steam as spring was ushered in. Jenny and Tom saw blossoms on early flowering trees around campus and notices of a rally sponsored by the coalition.

They got a bite to eat after church and arrived early at the site of the rally. They noticed a lot of campus and city police, as well as a few students with screen doors. Strange!

At the rally, which filled the courtyard, speakers urged solidarity with South African blacks and divestment of university holdings. Tom and Jenny heard the first two speeches and were getting ready to leave when a commotion to their right, on the sidewalk near the street, caught their attention. Several men and women were hammering a number of the screen doors together, and others were stapling plastic to the edges of the whole thing.

The police were moving toward the emerging structure when the speaker at the PA system announced, "Here is our Soweto, our Crossroads! This Branford shantytown will remain a symbol for us, until the board and administration decide to divest!"

One policeman grabbed a piece of plastic, evidently to tear it. That was all Jenny and Tom could see in the confusion. Surprised and a little frightened, they moved away from the activity just as everyone else seemed to be moving toward it.

As they walked back to their apartment, they could hear sirens of police cars in the distance. Excited and worried at the possibility of violence at Branford, they turned on the radio. An announcer said students had erected a shantytown, and police were waiting for a university decision about what to do with it. The television news that evening featured a university spokesperson, the Director of Public Information, who said a small group of students had illegally vandalized the campus and urged them to go home and to disassemble the makeshift structures immediately. A spokesperson for the coalition, who explained she was not the leader but a "temporary facilitator," said the shantytown would stay until three conditions were met: the university board meeting the next day would have to consider the overwhelming majority opinion at Branford for divestment of institutional holdings in South Africa–related companies, new investments must be stopped in such companies, and a schedule of gradual divestment established.

The late-night television news showed pictures of the university president speaking to the demonstrators in the dusk of Sunday evening. "You did not receive permission to do this," he said. "You are acting in a fashion contrary to the central mission of Branford—and all universities. This should be a place for healthy debate, but you are acting by force to cut off debate. Please desist and go home." However, the university granted permission for the shanties to remain until the board meeting, at which members of the coalition would be permitted to speak.

At the highly publicized board meeting the next day, six students did indeed speak, and university officials said they would consider the matter. That evening the television news covered large demonstrations at several campuses across the country, and there was word of the arrest of several hundred students at other shantytowns in those colleges and universities.

On Monday evening, after receiving news of the meeting, Tom White visited the shantytown and talked with several of its residents. The original structures had been augmented; now six or seven small rooms, made mostly of doors, were linked by polyethylene sheets, some of which were quite tattered. The whole place smelled of orange peels, and some of the students looked weary.

"We're being careful not to have leaders," they explained. "That way the administration must deal with the issues and with us all." Tom learned that members of the board, with few exceptions, had no knowledge of the most basic arguments—they were still ignorant of the Sullivan Principles, for example, and of the extent of transnational involvement in the economics of gold, diamonds, and chromium pricing and mining.

Tom told Jenny of his conversation with the demonstrators and of his sympathy with their attempts to get Branford University to divest. "Maybe it's not perfect," he said, "but it seems the best place for me to help right now." Jenny said she would like to go with him the following evening to learn more about the shantytown and the hopes of the protesters.

The newspaper on Tuesday morning carried the headline, BRANFORD STUDENTS ARRESTED, SHANTYTOWN DESTROYED. According to the story, seventy-plus students, mostly undergraduates, and about ten nonstudents had been arrested at 4:30 A.M. The plastic and wood structures had been leveled.

Tom took a test that day in his torts course, "a prelude to the final," according to the professor. He knew he had not done as well as usual on it, distracted as he was by his concern for the demonstrators and lacking his normal amount of preparation. His grades would influence heavily the decision as to whether he would help lead the *Branford Law Review* next year, his final year of study. Typically, law students who had been editors of the *Review* were offered the best jobs at graduation.

On his way to the library early Wednesday morning, Tom White saw several of the students he had met at the shantytown. "Where are you going?" he asked. They were on their way to join some others to sit at the administration building, requesting dismissal of the charges against those arrested the previous morning and serious consideration of the issue of divestment. Tom joined them in their walk and sat with them on the porch of the administration building. Almost immediately several policemen blocked the sidewalk. They could hear voices and people moving around the corners of the building also.

"They're sitting by each door," one of the students explained to Tom. "We have one group trying to get into the Office of New Investments too, for a sit-in there."

Tom, uneasy to be part of so organized a demonstration, now saw another group marching up the street, evidently from the freshman quadrangle. There appeared to be several faculty members and some fellow graduate students from the law school. About thirty of the hundred or more people collecting now sat on the sidewalk side of the police, who were sandwiched between two groups of polite but insistent demonstrators.

At this point a woman ran around from the other side of the building and shouted, "They said leave the treasurer's entrance in five minutes or be arrested!" She was out of breath, from both the excitement and the running. The group Tom had joined began to discuss moving, so they all could be arrested together.

"Rumor has it they might use the Chatham scenario this time," one member said. That action by the university had been formed a decade previously in the midst of Vietnam War protests. It consisted of arresting and expelling those who "inhibit normal processes of education."

Tom listened intently as he considered what to do. He knew most of the group had already decided to join those threatened with detention. However, the protesters would have to move around to be at the other door. What about the sidewalk sitters in front of them and those milling around? Tense and confused, he tried to make a decision.

### Discussion Notes

This case was described to me by a friend involved in one university's struggle with issues about divestment in companies doing business in the Republic of South Africa. Though I have disguised the situation, my friend told me that my account accurately reflects and truthfully represents the issues. The timeline has been given in almost precise detail; I dearly hope the situation in South Africa has changed dramatically for the better by the time the case is discussed.

This example has been used to help Christians concentrate on serious national and international issues. Naturally, Tom and Jenny White bring particular perspectives as Christians. What information does the case provide concerning their understanding of the Christian faith? What else would it be helpful to know regarding their religious perspectives?

Typically, a case discussion of Branford Shanty involves identification of the major characters, naming and discussing issues involved, dialogue concerning alternatives for Tom White at this point, and exploration of the reasons and consequences of each alternative.

Also helpful, because the case is complex and the issues so important, might be an invitation to members of the class to read other materials. The Minutes of the 197th General Assembly (1985), Presbyterian Church (U.S.A.), pp. 228–231, offers a recent opinion on the responsibilities of Christians in America to be involved in the issues of southern Africa. "Declaration of Conscience on South Africa and Namibia" has been reprinted from the UP-CUSA General Assembly Minutes (1981) and is available as a pamphlet.

# PART ONE

# Questions About Christian Living

# 1

# What Shall I Do?

This is the question of a man who met Jesus: "What shall I do to inherit eternal life?" You remember that encounter, reported in Luke 18:18–30. As Jesus "explained" the way God works, he pointed to God's power to save people, even wealthy ones. That was quite a feat, Jesus joked with the disciples, like helping a great camel to get through the eye of a needle.

The Gospels are full of such encounters. Disciples, crowds, and individual strangers all asked Jesus what they should do. Jesus was forever telling them, sometimes with stories, sometimes with riddles, and sometimes with what we call "hard sayings."

Among the stories, for example, look at the one about the Good Samaritan (Luke 10:25–37). There another person, a lawyer, had asked the same question. Jesus replied with the story about a man who fell among thieves. A priest and a Levite, both professionally religious, passed by. But a lowly Samaritan helped the victim. Jesus told the man to go and do likewise.

Among the teachings that seem to be riddles are those such as "Leave the dead to bury their own dead" (Luke 9:60). Jesus also told his disciples to leave their families and, in at least one account, to "hate them." Jesus' own behavior and his other teachings show care for grieving ones and for his family. So what did he mean? We wrestle with interpretations of the riddles.

Especially hard to hear are those sayings about God's judgment of the rich, of the people around Jesus, his generation, and the world. Personally, the account of the Judgment Day in Matthew 25 is the most memorable and riveting. However, look at Luke chapter 12 for another hard saying: "Sell your possessions, and give alms; provide yourselves with purses that do not grow old, with a treasure in the heavens that does not fail, where no thief approaches and no moth destroys. For where your treasure is, there

will your heart be also" (Luke 12:33–34). If we keep reading, we
see more such teachings about readiness for the kingdom and
preparation for its dawning.

As part of Christ's risen body the church, we know that God's
grace alone can save us. We cannot "earn" salvation. Further, most
of us probably would not want any salvation so paltry that we
could buy it. Remember the joke by Mark Twain: "I never would
be a member of a club that stooped so low as to admit me"?

Never mind, we do not have that choice. Moreover, the overwhelming gifts of God, through the death and resurrection of Jesus
Christ, made such a point clearly: the God who created the world
redeems it through Christ.

In Christian life we learn of God's gifts and how great they are.
God created, God sustains, God redeems us. We believe in Jesus
Christ. We depend upon God's Spirit to keep us.

As we sense gratitude, we praise God. At least in our healthier
times our praise to God outdistances all other expressions of our
life. We thank God for family and friends, for work and support
in doing it, for healing and comfort, for the hope of resurrection,
for all God's many gifts in our behalf.

For us in that posture of praise, this increases rather than dimin-
ishes the urgency of the question, What shall I do, what shall I
render to the Lord?

It is the response to that question, from whatever posture we ask
it, that defines Christian ethics. Christian ethics is more than just
a study of moral choices, even a study of improving the quality of
moral decisions. It is the study of active discipleship, the following
of the God we love.

"Lord, I want to be a Christian in my heart." That spiritual
springs to our lips not only for its compelling melody but also for
its haunting affirmation. It urges us by the very words of praise to
become what we claim to be. "I want to be more loving." "I want
to be like Jesus." Yes, but how?

> How shall I be more loving? How shall I be like Jesus?
> How shall I respond to God's gifts?
> How shall I grow in the Christian faith?
> How shall I proclaim the gospel "inna my heart," in my life?
> How can I discern God's Spirit at work in the world for
> healing and peace?

Naturally, as these questions quickly show, Christian ethics also
involves stewardship, evangelism, pastoral care, and spiritual de-

velopment. Life really is one fabric, and the Christian faith treats it as one.

Moreover, these questions so far are phrased in the singular: "I." We know so much more of our Christian life remains "we" than ever can be said in an "I." "What shall I do?" That question is almost always tied to—even taken from—"What shall we do?"

We, the family
We, the friends, the congregation
We, the community, the nation
We, the whole church universal
We, human beings

This mix of the "I" with all the "we's" of which we are a part leads to serious conflicts. In the Branford Shanty case, we see the problem of Tom White. But his problem is tied to problems of those around him, of institutions, of nations, and of people in the Republic of South Africa, black and white. People and institutions throughout the world are involved in apartheid, as all are involved in denial of human rights wherever that occurs in the world. Branford University, owning stocks and bonds of companies deeply involved in South Africa, is complicit in South African economic and political life. But even if Branford (or the Presbyterian Church, or any other institution) owned no stocks (or possessed no shares in companies far from South African involvement), Tom White and other Christians would still be involved when denial of human rights occurred there.

## What Is an Ethical Decision?

There is just one, albeit simple, example of Christian social ethics in which believers ask "What shall I do?" We make ethical decisions. This casebook presents situations that call for such decisions. But decisions are not the only center of the Christian life. Moreover, those decisions we can name and remember form a very small part of the decisions we make.

When was the last time you made an ethical decision? Most of us consider only the momentous, obviously courageous stands we take to be ethical. We put thought and prayer into making those decisions, and we sometimes pay a heavy price for taking them.

On the other hand, we make scores of decisions each day. And many more unthinking actions we take amount to actual decisions.

As a young boy growing up in Memphis, Tennessee, in the early

1950s, I made an ethical decision each time I rode the bus—which happened a lot in those days. As one labeled "white" in America, I took my seat in the front of the bus, never even thinking about it. When another white person, an older woman, was left standing as I sat, I barely had to think to decide to let her have my seat. I had been "raised right," as novelist Ferrol Sams says. I jumped up, and I gave her the place to sit.

Did I ever give my place to an older woman who was black? I swear I do not remember, though after 1955 I learned that Mrs. Rosa Parks was tired when she got on that bus in Montgomery, Alabama. She had sick members of her family, and she cared for several of them. She also had worked hard all day at demeaning, low-paying labor. I realize there are many women, and not a few men black and white, who would appreciate the seat given lightly by a healthy young person. I made many ethical decisions on Memphis buses, as did thousands of other riders in those days.

Now when I take public transportation I think about the ethical decisions involved—or at least I think about black people and tired people a lot more. As a white middle-class American of the 1980s, I rarely take public transportation. Only when gasoline became a political issue in the 1970s did I realize the use of this finite resource presented occasions for ethical decision making. Usually the car did not have a full load of people, nor does it now. Yet I used energy resources, "voted" with my body against providing better public transportation, and limited my opportunities to make focused decisions about where and when to sit on buses.

I do recall some deliberate, absorbing decisions. When my wife and I served in Zaire in the mid-1960s as missionaries, for example, we debated the risks and benefits of an invitation to drive a truck-load of young people to a youth conference in another region of the country. The young people belonged to a tribe that had been at war with the people of the tribe where we were going. Zairean friends urged us to make the trip, take the young people, and help overcome group fears. "The youngsters are members of one church with the others," they told us.

We took the truck, loaded with young people, and enjoyed the trip very much. It may even have given some help to Zairean Christians seeking reconciliation. The point here is that we made a conscious decision, and then we carried out what we decided.

Most of us call this second type of decision "ethical." In this casebook, for discussion and to sustain interest, most of the situations will be of this second type—"big" decisions. But the little ones are closely related to the ones we consider big. After all, Rosa Parks turned a little decision into a very big one just by sitting where she sat.

What is an ethical decision? It is a choice made, little or big. It means a moral choice, for it contrasts with an "unethical" or "immoral" decision. At the same time, the field of Christian ethics includes consideration of the wrong as well as of the right. My ethical decisions made out of habit on Memphis buses were shallow and simply followed a social pattern. At the same time, such decisions are subject to consideration here. We look at the less responsible, the less adequate, as well as the more appropriate responses to situations.

## A Look at History

Ever since the time of disciples and apostles, Christians have tried to respond to the gospel in living. Slaves, aristocrats, priests, farmers, merchants, and everyone else addressed Christian ethics. Early Christians made up books of rules and answers to particular problems, for example. Over time, they took resources from other traditions, especially from Greek philosophy and Roman law. Roman law based decisions of courts on certain principles, and Christians developed many important principles for behavior. Greek philosophy, which by the way contributed the very word "ethics" to the Christian vocabulary, emphasized certain virtues that Christians came to consider important alongside the ones in scripture.

Every age has had deep questions and hard issues to examine. What happens if a Christian is married to a person of another faith? What if a Christian breaks the law? How purely does a Christian have to live in order to remain in the church? Can a Christian go to war? If so, when? If not, what does the Christian do? Rule books and codes with the penalties for breaking laws became refined. As religious "orders" developed, special rules for them did too—for monks, nuns, friars, and even hermits. Scholastics brought all arenas of human knowledge to bear on issues in ethics.

Protestant reformers emphasized again the force and scope of the Christian gospel. God saved us because God gave faith; through God's grace came salvation. But the reformers, too, faced ethical dilemmas and sought to interpret rules and mores, with lots of Protestant rule books and codes of penalties resulting as well.

Principles have varied through the centuries, but several obviously exercise enormous influence for Christians in each age. Usually theologians have argued that Christian ethics formed a coherent "system." In recent centuries, as contact increased with other living religions, Christian ethicists frequently sought to prove that the Christian system surpassed other religious ethics.

During the twentieth century, a real debate has taken place among ethicists who thought the world was improving and others who pointed to pervasive human sinfulness. Another debate has run between those who emphasize the rules and principles for Christian life and those who say the relative nature of rules is more important. The second group has pointed to the importance of every situation in determining Christian response.

Most recently, a number of ethicists have said the basis of moral theology lies in the building of Christian character, not in either rules or analysis of discrete situations to locate responses. They have pointed to the drawing power of images for Christians, even in works of fiction.

A good text in Christian ethics points to the merits of each of these perspectives, and we do not have the space even to summarize that train of thought. However, we can see that our struggle to behave as Christians takes place in "a cloud of witnesses." We can learn from the classic ways of considering ethics. Typically, such ways take apart decisions and acts to examine their parts: looking at motive, intentions, the acts themselves, and at consequences, for example.

What are the *motives* of a Christian? What moves (even compels) us to do things? Are Christian motives different from the motives of other human beings? How conscious are we of motives? Do we choose among various motives, or are we motivated primarily by intuitions? In the Branford Shanty case, the motivations of Tom and Jenny White are not listed, but we can certainly name some: they want to help other people, for example; they are moved by human poverty and oppression; they also seem influenced by the concerns of other Christians. What motivations can you name in this general fashion? What motives are particularly tied to Tom's actions in the demonstration?

A second element, *intention,* asks about the aim of an action. What does the person or community want to help (or even make) happen? Again, intentions can be subconscious ones, which Christians try to bring to the surface for examination. Some intentions can be clearly stated, and they appear rational as well as viable for Christians.

Tom White obviously intends to have the Branford administration focus on the issue of disinvestment. More broadly, he intends to have moral considerations affect investment policy within the school. These obvious intentions are supplemented by others, some stated and some implied. The demonstrators want to cause disruption. They want to interrupt normal activity. What other intentions can you discern? What else is mentioned as intention?

Third, the *behavior* itself can be inspected. Sitting in a public place is quite different from throwing rocks there or shooting a gun at people. But the sitting might not be in a public place. It might take place on private property, interpreted by law as trespassing. Analysis of the actual behavior, and the limits of behavior, informs traditional ethics.

Fourth, the study of *consequences* has been followed in ethics. What are the results of certain actions, and how widely will the consequences be felt? How are consequences related to the other elements—to motivations, intentions, and actions?

In the Branford Shanty case, those questions Tom White phrases in the introduction mostly address this part of ethics. What other questions should he ask about consequences? Again, various levels of consequence come to bear, for some may be unforeseen and others obvious.

## Christian Principles and Human Situations

There is one briefly put way of examining a moral decision. You can see that it helps to consider the parts of a dilemma, though the whole is more than the sum of the parts. In addition, the Christian has no special claim to this way of proceeding. The focus on Christian principles and the emphasis on situations are both attempts to help Christians in their living.

Historically, most Christian ethics have focused on the norms, rules, and principles that the faith seeks (or even demands). "Love one another as I have loved you" (John 15:12) is just one of the principles received from scripture. These words of Jesus, remembered by the early church, were to rule actions within the community of the faithful and more broadly as well.

Several of the central principles we find in the Ten Commandments. Others we see in Old and New Testament passages at the core of the witness of scripture. "Remember the sabbath day, to keep it holy" (Ex. 20:8), for instance, led to many other rules about worship and restraint from regular work. When Jesus picked grain on a Sabbath and religious leaders criticized him for it, he called attention to other principles that helped interpret his actions.

On the other hand, the same passage has been used to point to the import of situations. Jesus determined action on the basis of the particular needs of that moment, including the need to teach about ethics. At least, that is the way other ethicists perceive the story of the picking of grain. They point to the relative nature of reality, to the unique quality in real-life events, and to the balancing of different and conflicting rules and principles.

Among today's "rule"-oriented ethicists, Paul Ramsey claimed the Christian follows both general principles and what he termed "rules of practice." If keeping promises is a general rule for Christians, then in each promise-keeping occasion the Christian tries to make that action fit the general principle. A rule of practice conforms more specifically to habit and routine, governed by the general principle.

Among situation-oriented ethicists, Joseph Fletcher argued that Christians respond from love, not in a legalistic way. He saw principles so frequently conflicting that confusion resulted, and he wanted people to recognize the value of weighing alternatives in behalf of the most love for the greatest number of people. Fletcher saw rules other than "love for neighbor" as false absolutes. Justice, promises, even acts of love varied; the Christian should look at the individual situation in order to respond appropriately.

As situation-oriented Christians have accused rule-oriented Christians of being "legalists" and even "Pharisees," so the second group has accused the first of practically destroying a shared sense of ethics. The situationalists are just gentle anarchists, according to critics. In a debate that has proven to be a rather hot one at times, both perspectives have been presented as though Christians make decisions without both principles or situations in mind.

For the Branford Shanty case, the rule-oriented ethicist would look for governing principles for Tom White, the university, and the larger culture in the United States and in the world. Does his demonstrating break the law? Is the law constructive? Are the conflicting rules concerning love and justice overbearing and applicable? Then Christian action might realistically take place in a responsible manner.

The situationalist would consider this demonstration, compare the value of alternative actions for Tom White, and decide finally on the basis of expressions of greatest self-giving love for the most neighbors possible. Both kinds of ethics refer to parts already considered—to motives, intentions, the actions themselves, and their consequences.

Revival of earlier Christian emphases on community, values, and character influence ethics again in the 1980s. Ethicists who concentrate on these topics say they are more important today than the debate about method in earlier decades.

# 2

# How Do I Choose?

According to scripture, Joshua gathered the tribes of Israel at Shechem. All the representatives of the people "presented themselves before God." Joshua told them about God's faithfulness, reciting their story of preservation and the list of God's gifts to them. Then he called for a choice. "Now therefore fear the LORD. . . . And if you be unwilling to serve the LORD, choose this day whom you will serve . . . but as for me and my house, we will serve the Lord" (Josh. 24:14–15).

Evidently from year to year, or at least in times of crisis, the people of Israel reenacted this remembered time. Notice as you read the chapter that Joshua warned the leaders what a choice to follow the Lord would mean: putting away other, foreign gods and remaining faithful to the Lord God. That theme of choosing runs through all of scripture. Do those people whom God chooses have choices? What are they? What are the limits on these choices? How do freedom and discipline relate?

At one level, Christians certainly have choices. Consider Tom White in the Branford Shanty case. He can remain at his present location. He can go with those who join the ones threatened with arrest. Or he can simply walk away from the demonstration. What other choices can he make in this situation? What combinations of choices would seem to be present for him?

Few of us would question Tom White's ability at this point to choose among alternatives. His decision depends upon many things, but he does have a choice. Few would argue that Tom White has one way to respond and no others. With Christian integrity, he could take one or more of several actions.

At another level, though, Tom White cannot be absolutely free. He may even seem more bound than free. His commitments bind him at a number of points. He is a Christian, first of all, and a member of a community of Christians. His alternatives are also limited by responsibilities and relationships as a member of a family, as a spouse and potential father. As a member of a university community, he has also made promises about his behavior and committed himself to learning. Further, he seeks to engage in the profession of law, where standards of admission and standards of practice are supposed to be high ones. Though the text of the case does not specify, we can infer that other constraints limit Tom White's choices. His background, his psychological composition, the social environment all have an effect. A political and ethical demonstration in the 1980s is not as unusual as it would have been in American society in the 1950s, nor as common as in the late 1960s. Again, how shy or gregarious is he personally? How fearful or excited does he become at the sight of large numbers of police officers? All these factors exert an influence on him.

Thus Tom White does have choices, but his choices are limited. After looking at the nature of the gospel and at the life of the Christian in action, it makes sense to examine the nature of choices and the communities that help form and limit those choices.

Today we assume that choices are almost always available for people. In fact, one criticism of modern culture speaks of a paralysis of most people today who are baffled by the range of alternatives set before us. The speed of change and the variety among possibilities causes a shock that simply overcomes some people. It would seem that Christians, free in Jesus Christ for activity in the world, would have resources in the face of bewilderment. But we frequently hesitate in action—do we not?—perhaps in shock at the range of possibilities.

It seems ironic that people outside the Christian movement, especially those who know little of Reformed Christianity, accuse us of fatalism. *Que será será,* "What will be will be," is a nice lyric, but it makes absolutely no sense for Christian ethics. The doctrine of predestination, so central in much of Reformed theology, has not encouraged Christians to surrender choices. Rather, it has provided assurance that God cares for people, that God cares for us, that God cares for each of us and all of us together. God uses human beings, even those who do not know they are doing God's will, on behalf of God's purpose.

God works in and through the world, through people, and especially through the church. God turns the poor choices we make into ways of accomplishing the divine will. That does not excuse us from trying as best we can to be faithful, to follow God's direction. We try to remain faithful in choosing, but we remember the comfort that Joseph, son of Jacob, provided his repenting brothers: "Fear not . . . you meant evil . . . but God meant it for good" (Gen. 50:19–20). We also remember the gospel, that even while we are yet sinners Christ died for us.

Choices. That we make them seems obvious. How we make them seems much harder to tell. Do we reason out our choices? What part do our communities play? Can we grow in weighing choices and deciding wisely? To look at these questions, we will consider community and character building in this chapter. We will look at some images of the Christian life and at insights about growth in chapters 3 and 4.

## Community and Commitment

Tom and Jenny White joined the Presbyterian Church when they moved to the Branford area. Their participation in a Christian community seems to have been quite natural. For Presbyterians, as for most other Christians, participation in a congregation also means sharing in the whole body of Christ throughout the world. Thus they belong to a distinct, particular Christian community, but also to a denomination of which that congregation is part. They also belong to the ecumenical community, both local and world-wide.

The community influences them enormously; a little of that influence shows in the text of the case. Worship draws the congregation together, offering hymns, reading and interpreting scripture, a greeting of sisters and brothers with "kindred minds," a whole range of prayers to God, and so forth. That congregation offers a "tie that binds our hearts in Christian love," to use the words of the hymn. Even if the Whites are so busy with work they miss a worship service, or if they visit kin elsewhere, or if they are ill, they are still part of that worship and of the life of the congregation.

Notice the ways in which the congregation's life affected the situation in which Tom White finds himself. Where did they hear speeches about South Africa? Who did the speakers represent to them? What other influences can be named from the text? What can be inferred?

Ethicists speak of Christians as bearing a "fellowship ethic," a *"koinonia* ethic" that helps form the conscience of each member. For lifelong Christians, such a fellowship begins even before they can recognize it. The relations continue through thick and thin, through Sunday school teachers, friends from church, and the examples of ministers and other leaders.

For those who become Christian and join the church later in their lives, the community has been at work even before their "decision." The congregation joined has witnessed, shown itself in behalf of the gospel, to the one saying yes. In the words of Stanley Hauerwas, an ethicist who stresses the importance of community for commitment (*The Peaceable Kingdom,* p. 62), "Christian ethics begins in a community that carries the story of the God who wills us to participate in a kingdom established in and through Jesus of Nazareth."

The Whites not only joined the church in the Branford area, they also registered to vote. Tom enrolled as a student in a university law school there, and Jenny started teaching school in a particular school system. In brief, they joined a number of other overlapping and sometimes competing institutional communities. In addition, as you can see from the text, they both made friends and formed informal social communities.

Tom and Jenny White form a community, too, along with their parents and the children they have or adopt. A wider network of relatives usually surrounds the central family: aunts and uncles, cousins, nieces and nephews, and so on. Here, too, ties "bind" almost everyone with celebrations and the markings of passages among those relatives.

Examination of who we are as Christians also involves us in looking carefully at the communities in which we participate. What are the ties that bind in other communities, as worship and educational activities bind our hearts within a congregation?

In the area of the country where I live, the sport of basketball provides a binding tie. To belong to any of the local university communities seems to mean knowing about the teams, going to games, and cheering for the team. People who are not teachers, staff, or students at the various schools are still tied to the place by identifying with one or more of the teams. Such an emphasis may be recreational, even therapeutic. It can also prove detrimental for many people. It may drive people to neglect other communities. Friends joke that it may become idolatrous. Consider other ties among communities—for they are certainly there.

Can a Christian exist without belonging to a congregation? Theoretically, yes. One can remember communities of Christians or look forward to occasions of gathering and sharing. But in practice, the community is part and parcel of real Christian life.

Hauerwas and others who study ethics say that our commitments are born within communities and tied closely to those networks of other people. If we expect others to live in peaceful ways, for example, and we grow from others expecting us to do likewise, we become more deeply committed to peace. More, we can learn from the ways in which living communities of Christians have practiced peaceful living, and we can see how commitments are shared. Specifically, Hauerwas speaks of his own growth in commitment to peace through sharing learning communities and experiences with John Howard Yoder and other Christian people.

Assessing the commitments and the communities, according to many ethicists today, helps more than just considering particular decisions and the situations that surround them.

How deep do our commitments to members of the family lie? How strong are the ties to members of the congregation in which we participate? What commitments do we have to justice? How widely do those commitments extend? Are hungry people to be fed? All of them? Everywhere? Examination of these commitments usually finds them growing out of a shared life. I would argue that even when we cannot locate the source of such commitments in communities we have shared, they certainly have come out of those communities nonetheless.

## Character and Ethics

The cases in Part Two give some information about the communities and commitments of the people involved. I hope you will plumb the stories and discuss these communities and commitments as well as consider the decisions to be made. The cases also give information about the protagonists' values and about their character. Values and character frequently are ignored today, but both need attention and study.

The story is told that Sam Ervin, the Senator from North Carolina who chaired the Watergate hearings, was asked about the "tremendous weight" of public expectation concerning his leadership. He responded in humility, according to a witness, that he was ready for the responsibility. "I've been preparing for this moment all my life," he said.

This Christian leader—who, by the way, was a Presbyterian—certainly conducted himself as chairman with dignity, a sense of fairness, and a sense of vision. People who followed the hearings closely commented frequently on the character that Sam Ervin exhibited.

"Character" is really a difficult thing to talk about, impossible fully to explain. Dictionaries frequently speak of it as "the ethical structure of a person," or "ethical strength." Karen Labacqz speaks of character as the "inside view" of what is right on the part of a mature person. Stanley Hauerwas says to develop character means a person becomes a responsible agent in ethical matters, not just doing right things but in a sense "being" right. According to this perspective, Sam Ervin in a delicate and burdensome situation acted with integrity and maturity because he had character. He could say, "I did that," and know who the "I" really was.

Ethicists who look at the character of people in Christian ethics also talk about the developing of virtues. Paul, you know, spoke of both virtues and vices. He praised faith, hope, and love, but declared love was the greatest (1 Corinthians 13). He also encouraged Christians to overcome vices (Ephesians 4). Others in the Bible had much to say about both virtues and vices.

As Christianity became more organized, leaders took from Greek thought the study of virtues and vices. Virtues that had been important for the Greeks—prudence, for example—came also to be seen as Christian. In the Middle Ages, the church came to name seven virtues: wisdom, justice, courage, temperance, along with faith, hope, and love. They also named seven particularly deadly vices: pride, envy, sloth, anger, avarice, gluttony, and lust. In different Christian traditions the lists might vary, but usually these were the ones included. Whatever the list, those who would develop as Christians sought to increase the measure of virtues and decrease the hold of vices.

Identifying virtues and vices might lead to taking certain actions or avoiding other actions, but the primary focus remained on the person, not on the behavior. What is a Christian? Who is a Christian? We know the Christian is not just a person who does things a certain way. No, a Christian centers upon God, who has redeemed and will redeem us. In responding to the gospel, the Christian grows in character. To grow in character, one can develop the virtues and diminish the vices—seek to become more just, wiser, more loving.

Most of us find it easier to discuss cases and Christian action than to discuss the building of character and the holding of the faith that God will enable us to grow in Christ. Especially when a book like this one gives cases to examine, we are tempted to weigh the merits of actions. However, the cases also give us information about the people involved, and we can practice thinking about character, moral agency, and the nurture of virtues along the way.

To remind ourselves one more time: God gives us everything. God gives the faith, the virtues, the reasoning ability, and the sense of purpose in living. The Christian is one who is spiritually growing in Christ. In the words of the apostle, "I have been crucified with Christ; it is no longer I who live, but Christ who lives in me" (Gal. 2:20). That is a typical statement of Paul, and we hear it echoed through the ages. Call it mystical, call it religious experience, call it what you will. It is the core of the Christian—a transcendent and immanent sense of God's presence. Honestly, it does yield action. Jesus said, "Not every one who says to me, 'Lord, Lord,' shall enter the kingdom of heaven, but he who does the will of my father who is in heaven" (Matt. 7:21). God gives that discipleship, and we are the disciples.

One Sunday in his sermon, our minister quoted Dietrich Bonhoeffer: "The sin of respectable people is running away from responsibility." Amen! I thought of Bonhoeffer's insight into how much grace costs and that cheap grace is none at all. Discipleship comes from disciples, from Christians with character who try to follow Jesus Christ. Such gifts from God are not magically given at baptism, they are provided through God's giving us ability to grow, to nurture, to expect the kingdom dawning.

## What Is a Case?

The relationship of receiving God's vision for ourselves and the world, while responding in discipleship and seeking to grow in character, is a deep subject. I hope you reflect on that relationship in your discussions, and that the cases do more than just lead you to looking at actions of Christians. To speak of cases, let me explain about the ones provided here.

In this book, a case is a written account of an actual situation in the lives of people. Some of you who use the book may be very familiar with this kind of example, used particularly in several forms of professional education. Others of you may be familiar with other forms of case study: the use of verbatims in psychology, or of case histories in social work, for example. The purpose of the case is to begin with the instance and to move from that specific example to learn of other situations and resources in more general terms.

I have disguised most of the cases, so people could share their experiences without embarrassment and so I would not be meddling in the privacy of some people without permission. Each time, I gave to the person sharing the case with me a draft of my effort to write about that experience. And each time, one or more participants said the written presentation represented accurately the issues at stake.

You will notice that the cases view the world from one person's point of view, rather than assuming the feelings and perceptions of all the characters. This limited perspective simulates the way each of us encounters things. We can imagine what other people think and feel, but we are not quite sure. In this respect a case of this kind differs from most fiction, which assumes an omniscient perspective. When you study the case, it makes sense to begin with the presenting character and try to sympathize—or empathize—with him or her. Since the book is offered especially for men's study groups in the church, most of the cases offer a male perspective from which to begin.

Naturally, such cases have limits. At times, readers must infer information I do not give. To discuss what needs to be known for decision also helps us see what we think important in given situations. Readers have to suspend disbelief, at least temporarily, to study these cases. I have tried them all out with study groups, and at least with those groups the disguises did not inhibit this process.

For more than a decade now, colleagues in many denominations have been offering these kinds of cases for Christian education. Most of the ones I have written, and most done by friends and colleagues, have been for the education of seminary students. We have published several casebooks in such areas as Bible, church history, systematic theology, ethics, and administration. Adult classes studying these seminary cases have enjoyed a number of them. Members have urged us to write more for general church use. The cases offered here may lack some of the technical data provided in those meant for seminary classes, but they maintain the same style and point to similar dilemmas.

Study of these cases assumes that we have choices in ethical situations, that we can learn from discussion with other Christians, and that we can gain skills in bringing Christian resources to bear on the decisions we make. Case study also assumes God's Spirit at work among us and within us, showing us ways to grow in the faith and ways to proclaim the gospel in our lives.

We have choices in tight spots, where Christian values and models are at stake. I am fascinated at the way most of us, thinking abstractly, consider one response "right" and others "wrong." Yet in real situations, complex and personal the way Branford Shanty was for Tom White, we can realize several possibilities for response. Some responses may be more adequate than others. Some ways of responding we may describe in terms of vices more than virtues—"the lazy way" or "a selfish response." Yet we can see several alternatives for White, defending at least some of them with reference to virtues and to Christian thought—"prudence would dictate" or "Christian hope leads to. . . ."

Even more, discussion of cases can help us. After fifteen years in case study, I am firmly convinced of its value. We can practice in the situations of others ways in which we respond, learning along the way from others—from their wisdom and their foolishness. Almost every case discussion leads participants to share similar quandaries.

Third, we can gain skills in bringing Christian resources to bear on our own situations. Christians have spoken generally of four groups of resources God provides: the Bible, the Christian tradition, personal resources such as conscience and reason, and the wisdom of others around us. We can bring all four kinds of resources to bear on human situations in case study.

# 3

# How Shall I Live?

There was a time, not too long ago, when things really pressed in on me. As a teacher in a seminary, I felt the need to learn more about the diversity of the church's life and to share that knowledge with students who prepare for ministry. I had some writing projects that begged for completion. Church groups graciously asked me to speak, teach, and learn among them. My wife's work seemed particularly demanding, and I wanted to support her in an important effort to help children in special education. Our teenagers required parental labor of a different kind from that to which I was accustomed—and my company at times had to be fitted to their busy schedules. These were all the usual pressures, and in big doses.

This is neither to brag nor complain about my situation at that point. Mostly I am grateful—for spouse and sons who care and are interested in others and in me, for work that remains a pleasure, for a sense of urgency about the gospel, for students and faculty colleagues who feed me as well as call upon me for aid, and for all the rest of a comfortable and interesting life. I realize the luxury of my situation, in a world in which worries about health, food, and security pervade the lives of many of us. I realize that most work, when folk can get it, can be dull or demeaning.

All the same, things were pressing in, and I discovered I was asking, How shall I live? How shall I do what I want, what is needed and expected of me? My roles as spouse, parent, minister, teacher, friend, and Christian all made demands on my time and energy. How could I sort them out?

The sense of being pressed soon passed, with counsel among friends and family, some sorting of priorities, and some reflection and prayer. It is indeed a gift to have faith that God provides us different ways to live, different callings, and different resources for our sustenance.

Traditional images of the Christian life helped me in responding to that question, How shall I live? We all have models that guide us, whether we consciously attend to them or not. In seeking to be Christian people, we naturally try to follow models and images we know.

Some of the best models come from scripture itself. The portrait of the people waiting for the wedding party, for example, helps immensely (Matthew 25). I think about that image when I become tired, or maybe just lazy. The image of the man who sold everything for the pearl of great price (Matthew 13) helps in a time of sorting out priorities.

Consider some of the images that inform your Christian life. One friend tells me about the power of the figure of Zacchaeus for her (Luke 19:1–10). That tax collector received Jesus joyfully. Out of his faith, Zacchaeus tried to overcome the wrongs he had done and to help the poor with half his wealth.

In all fairness, I should say some images in scripture are quite negative. For example, take the account of Ananias and Sapphira in Acts 5. They lied, and the disciples judged them harshly. "A great fear fell upon the whole church, and upon all who heard of these things," says the writer of Acts (5:11). That certainly is true for me!

What biblical images are available for perhaps influencing the actions of Tom White in the Branford Shanty case? The work of certain prophets comes to mind—Amos, for example, and Hosea. In one way, Tom might be seen as a disciple or see himself as one. What images might help him respond imaginatively to the situation? How do such images work on the human imagination?

Earlier in American Christianity, most people seemed more familiar with images from scripture than they do today. They would talk about friends as biblical characters—"She was Ruth to me," "He decided wisely, as Solomon," or "She is a true suffering servant." You can see the power of such images in the naming of children: for apostles, gospel writers, and family members of Jesus. That practice still continues, but frequently the reference seems oblique.

At any rate, several of the important images in scripture deserve attention as we study Christian decisions. The "saint," "the disciple," and the "pilgrim" can all describe the Christian. In addition, we can speak of "telling a story" and of being "born again" as descriptive of the Christian life. We can learn from all five of these images, and all are useful in studying the cases that follow.

## Am I a Saint?

The saint, or holy one, remains an important image in the Bible and throughout Christian history. It is easy for us to think about other people—very special ones—when we hear the word "saint"; Mother Teresa of Calcutta comes to mind first. Then I think of Martin Luther King, Jr., and Dietrich Bonhoeffer. (Maybe, as a Protestant, I'm saying to myself, "Catholics don't have all the saints.")

In the Bible, the word "saint" applies more broadly in both testaments. In the Old Testament, it applied most of the time to the whole of Israel. "You shall be holy," says the Leviticus code; "for I the LORD your God am holy" (19:2). Because God loved them, the people of Israel were "set apart" and consecrated (Deut. 33:3). Psalms, Daniel, and 2 Chronicles began to use the words "holy" and "saint" in a more restricted way sometimes, much as some Christian communities narrowed the use of the word at times in their history.

Paul loved the word "saint." He began letters—Romans, 1 Corinthians, Ephesians, Philippians, and others—by calling the Christians in those places "saints." (The English word "saint" is from the Latin *sanctus,* "holy one.") When people strayed from the "straight and narrow" (as Christians always do), Paul still called them saints. Only later did the word also come to mean those Christians in the first generations of the church (Jude 3).

In Christian history, the image of the saint has changed several times. In the sixth century, for example, people began to pray to the dead for healing. They focused prayers particularly on martyrs from their own age and from earlier generations of Christians. The word "saint" became closely connected with Christian martyrdom, for both Eastern and Western Christians. In the Middle Ages, warriors were particular candidates for sainthood. Later saints came to be associated with the newly forming nations of Europe. Tribes and peoples in other areas wanted their own saints, and even today a sense of sainthood is linked by Catholics with national identity.

All these later uses of the image of the saint catch part of the sense, but they seem to miss the full biblical meaning and the power of the phrase "communion of saints" in the early creeds. There, all the believers are saints, special indeed and "holy ones" through God's work in them.

Are we saints? According to the Bible and the early confessions of the church, the answer is yes. Those of us who are Protestant Christians try to recapture the original use of the image for a Christian. Many Catholic and Orthodox Christian leaders also move now toward that use of "saint."

Being saints does make us special—all of us. Many Protestants, especially in the tradition of John Wesley, have debated whether Christians can "become perfect" in living, as Jesus told people to do (Matt. 5:48). A more helpful tradition, at least for many who use this image, comes out of Christian concentration on gaining the virtue and overcoming the vices.

Protestants, paying attention more to the relationship of believers to God and to Jesus Christ than to the nurture of virtue, have not emphasized the increase of those attributes and the decrease in vice as much as we might. In Bunyan's *Pilgrim's Progress,* for example, Christian encounters fear and has Hopeful for a companion, but the deadly sins do not play a significant part, nor do the whole range of virtues.

Almost all writers agree it is more interesting to explore the vices than the virtues. In Christian ethics, however, we find great help in each of the seven virtues. Examining love and justice, their relation and their sometime competition for the Christian, has occupied both Paul Tillich and Reinhold Niebuhr, two major ethicists and theologians.

In Branford Shanty, we can see the attempt by Tom White to exercise wisdom and prudence but also to remain faithful. We can also see the vices at work, or at least the temptation to them, in his behavior. Such an analysis of our own behavior can yield insight and help in decision making.

## Am I a Disciple?

"Disciples" are mentioned a lot in the New Testament. Sometimes the reference is to one or another of the Twelve. More often, though, it simply means "believers in Jesus Christ," those who seek to follow him. The Gospel According to John makes the point clearly: "Jesus then said to the Jews who had believed in him, 'If you continue in my word, you are truly my disciples, and you will know the truth, and the truth will make you free' " (John 8:31–32).

The word "disciple" came to mean for many those who believed during Jesus' own lifetime. All the Gospels, as well as the book of Acts, use the word more inclusively. It really meant (and means) a pupil, one who learns from another. We who would learn from

Jesus are disciples, and this image, like that of saint, carries heavy consequences for us (and joyful results as well). Being a disciple implies having discipline. Jesus said that disciples would bear crosses, even as he bore a cross (Matt. 16:24). It meant forgoing home and family (Luke 14:26).

Sometimes Christian ethics has used the image of Jesus himself. "Be like Jesus," ethicists have urged us. More appropriate than that image, however, is this one of discipleship. I know I cannot be like Jesus, but I can certainly seek to follow, as other people did and do.

There are many disciplines related to the faith—prayer, self-denial, stewardship, study, and candor, to mention just a few. Take the matter of candor. What does it mean to tell the truth? How can we discipline ourselves in truth telling? What of our withholding the truth? Is that dishonest? Practice in telling the truth gives just one example of discipleship. What of secrets? What of innocent deceptions? What of lying to protect others? If we plumb this sensitive area of Christian living, we may see needs for ourselves, for the church, and for society.

Ethicist Sissela Bok, in her book *Lying,* offers a fine start for the Christian who would explore telling the truth. She delves into the nature of deception as it is practiced in America today. She speaks of deception in the political area. Do Presidents and members of Congress have the right to lie, or even the right to withhold the truth from one another, or from the American people? She says no, in almost every situation—and this was in 1978, long before the issues related to secret sales of arms became open problems.

Consider the seemingly healthy patient in a routine physical examination who is found to have a virulent strain of cancer, inoperable and probably deadly within six months. Should the physician report this to the patient immediately, even though the patient has told the doctor of a long-awaited week's vacation to be taken the next day? Further, should the physician discuss chemotherapy, knowing it will probably fail to prolong life and will increase the suffering?

To explore the nature of truth and the telling of it requires discipline. Bok concludes usually on the side of full, truthful disclosure in almost all private and all public situations. She even criticizes the social sciences for using placebos (sugar pills for control groups) in experimental situations. She also says scientists should not tell subjects they are working on one topic while really experimenting on something else.

We may conclude each probe in a different way from Bok, but

it helps us to look deeply into such matters. Listen to her pointing to avenues for helping (p. 243):

> Individuals, without a doubt, have the power to influence the amount of duplicity in their lives and to shape their speech and action. They can decide to rule out deception wherever honest alternatives exist, and become much more adept at thinking up honest ways to deal with problems. They can learn to look with much greater care at the remaining choices where deception seems the only way out. They can make use of the test of publicity to help them set standards to govern their participation in deceptive practices. Finally, they can learn to beware of efforts to dupe them, and make clear their preference for honesty even in small things.

## Am I a Pilgrim?

The image of the Christian as a pilgrim, a sojourner on the way but not yet home, has been important throughout the history of the church. If we are saints and disciples in some ways, we might also be pilgrims, but the image may seem foreign to many American Christians. We feel ourselves at home in the world—maybe too thoroughly. On the other hand, for most people, struggling to find food and grateful for meager clothing and shelter, such a picture of life can be easily grasped. In addition, Americans who move frequently from city to city or from farm to city seem to use the image to describe themselves.

In ancient Israel, the people traveled to holy places—to Bethel, Shiloh, Shechem, Gilgal, and other locations. According to the psalms (15, 24, 27, and several others) the person on pilgrimage tried to live in an upright manner. The morally pure person makes the proper pilgrim:

> Who shall ascend the hill of the LORD?
> And who shall stand in his holy place?
> He who has clean hands and a pure heart,
>     who does not lift up his soul to what is false,
>     and does not swear deceitfully.
>
>                                    (Psalm 24:3–4)

The trips to holy places evidently seemed more important than "clean hands" for many Israelites, because prophets and other reformers discouraged attention to hollow acts of piety. After the monarchy of David and Solomon, pilgrimages to Jerusalem became very important for the covenant people. After the upheaval of the Babylonian exile, the tradition was revived. The great Jerusalem Passover pilgrimage formed the context for Jesus' journey at the time of his crucifixion and resurrection.

Pilgrimages quickly became popular in Christianity too, and pilgrims kept going to Jerusalem because it was a sacred place for many. From the second century, acts of piety included journeys, and the life of the pilgrim became a model to be followed by Christians. In medieval times, Christians could receive indulgences if they traveled to places of martyrs and saints for blessings. In fact, the crusaders waged war to "free" Palestinian holy places from Islamic control in behalf of Christian pilgrims.

Historically, Protestant Christians generally resisted making pilgrimages, but the image of the Christian as a pilgrim continued to be powerful. John Bunyan's *Pilgrim's Progress* deeply influenced Reformed ethics and piety. In that well-known book the pilgrim Christian makes a journey to Celestial City, encountering all kinds of trials and tribulations on the way. Bunyan's hymn, "He who would valiant be 'gainst all disaster," portrays the pilgrim's journey in verse.

Basically, for Protestants the image has meant, in the words of another hymn, that "this world is not our home." Paul had spoken of earthly existence as living in a tent (2 Cor. 5:1). When the tent is destroyed, we will have a heavenly dwelling that will be our real home. "We would rather be away from the body and at home with the Lord" (v. 8).

The pilgrim recognizes that he or she is "on the way." This means that all sustenance for life is supplied by God through others. It means the pilgrim is a guest. Such an image can become distorted, and not too long ago some Protestant Christians emphasized this life as a "veil of tears." Today in the United States, however, we may need to reclaim and use such an image as "pilgrim" in order to see that ownership and wealth can be demonic images when they guide us in living. In American life, we are all children of pilgrim parents who migrated or moved, sometimes willingly and other times unwillingly; we also have Abraham as a sojourner and Christ as "the pioneer and perfecter of our faith" (Heb. 12:2), as the telling of our story continues.

## Am I Telling a Story?

According to Deuteronomy, the people of Israel, when called on to declare who they were in the presence of God, were supposed to tell their story, which recalled that God kept promises for them: "And you shall make response before the LORD your God, 'A wandering Aramean was my father; and he went down into Egypt and sojourned there, few in number; and there he became a nation'" (Deut. 26:5).

Israel explained the creation and the nature of human sin with a compelling story of God and original people in a primeval garden. The destruction of their kingdom was explained with stories of unfaithful leaders. The retaking of the land they told in story as the renewal of covenants.

According to the Acts of the Apostles, in the excitement of Pentecost, Peter rose to address the gathered crowd with a story about Jesus being the Christ. Again, as Paul explained to young churches what the Christian life implied, he used examples from his story and the stories of other Christians and reminded hearers of their stories as well. The Christian story is our source of meaning. We share the faith that at a particular time and place God became a human being, incarnate.

One of my favorite hymns, though I was embarrassed to admit it for a while, is the rousing "Tell Me the Old, Old Story." And that is the major Christian story—the one about Jesus and his love. We have to know the characters in that story to know who we are as Christians. The story is not first a story about ourselves. It is a story about God. However, it becomes a personal story as we profess Jesus Christ. Following our confession of faith, even before such a confession can be made in words, our lives tell the story of God's continuing care for the world and God's love for us.

Our lives "witness" to God's love and care. We *are* testimonies of a sort. What sort? In a prayer meeting in a holiness church, I chuckled when one man stood and said, "Lord, I've been perfect for the last six years. I got out of jail, and I haven't been back. I quit hurting people. I've been faithful to my wife, and I don't drink much anymore." I laughed until I wondered to myself what testimony I could make. My problems in Christian living are not the ones he mentioned, at least I do not think they are. But can people seeing me at work know God loves them? Seldom, I confess.

Two friends, Oliver Williams and John Houck, wrote a study book for Christian business people called *Full Value.* They put the matter of stories this way (p. 12):

> The actions of a Christian do not really flow from *principles;* rather they flow from *stories,* and in particular the story of Jesus as por-

trayed in the New Testament. The "story" concept helps us see that our principles ("Love your neighbor") and values (community, honesty) acquire a definite sense from their context. For this reason the Christian values revealed in the Bible are usually set in the context of a story or event that Jesus used to teach his disciples.

## Am I Born Again?

In telling of God's kingdom dawning, we are telling not only the old story but a new story as well. Our part in that new story begins with new birth.

In recent years one image has been really loaded with feeling, both positive and negative. "Have you been born again?" is to some Christians an invitation to communion and to others an invitation to fight. As with the other images—saint, disciple, pilgrim, story-teller—the image of the Christian as born again has roots in scripture.

According to John, a Pharisee named Nicodemus came to see Jesus at night. He told Jesus that he believed him to be a teacher from God. Jesus responded by telling Nicodemus that only those born anew (or from above) could see the kingdom of God. Nicodemus asked how that was possible, and Jesus answered, "Truly, truly, I say to you, unless one is born of water and the Spirit, he cannot enter the kingdom of God" (John 3:5). Jesus went on to teach about the difference between earthly life and heavenly life.

Some Protestants, and a small percentage of Catholics, say that baptism of the Spirit is different from regular baptism and must be present for believers to have full gifts of the Spirit. Some even say that until a person speaks in tongues the second baptism has not occurred, and they cite accounts of Pentecost to prove their case. But the great majority of Christians through the ages have interpreted this image of being born again as a reference to baptism. It is the introduction of the Christian into the faith, and the baptism is a sign and symbol of rebirth. In the words of scripture and liturgy, one becomes dead to sin and alive in Christ Jesus our Lord.

In the more inclusive way of interpreting the image, we are all "born again," and we rejoice in our baptism and faith. That image opens us to understand that we are all children in the Christian faith, seeking to grow into the fullness of Christ.

# 4

# How Shall I Grow?

Our neighbors have two little boys, ages four and two. You can imagine our delight at watching these children and their friends at play. It brings back memories of when our own were those ages, and when parenting seemed more active than it is now for us. Both boys are learning like crazy! We can see them grow each week. Two months ago the four-year-old began riding a bike on his own. Both can throw balls now, farther and farther. They talk more readily with others, and their interests widen all the time.

It is particularly fun to watch the younger right now. He is just learning to distance himself from the four-year-old. Sometimes he will mimic his brother mercilessly. If the older takes a stone and throws it, the younger will do exactly the same. If the older yells, the younger will try to use the same voice. If the older runs through our garden . . . well, you get the picture.

We can sometimes see the younger boy marching to a different drummer. The older will play in the sandpile, and the younger will stray into forbidden heaps of dirt where a house is being built. The older will throw a ball, and the younger will give it studied neglect instead of retrieving it as before. The mother or father will call both, and the younger will move in an opposite direction from the older. As both children learn to live, through the church they attend, their Christian faith is growing also. In many ways we all continue to learn like those youngsters, both following models and distancing ourselves from them, as well.

In the congregation where I first learned about faith, I remember a gentle man my parents respected. He sold cars, and they said he told the truth "anyway." (I later came to understand more fully what they meant.) At any rate, though he merely attended church in my presence (or I in his), Mr. Wellford exercised a great influence upon me. He would remember my name, ask me how things were going, and—when I sat far away from my parents—pass me a hymnbook with the page already turned.

I remember all kinds of people at that church—some talked too much, some prayed really simple prayers which I sensed to be real, some made no sense, some told me Bible stories that helped me immensely. I recall a man who mistreated his family, as I learned from his daughter. And there was a woman who lived through severe trials with courage and grace. Another woman looked down her nose at me. Lots of grown-ups and children influenced me. My coming of age in the Christian faith, my learning to try to follow Jesus Christ, remains tied to all those people and many more I cannot remember.

My faith is affected by many factors, only some of which I recognize. My ethical sensibilities and my decision making are likewise affected by certain people and events. I find it helpful to study those ingredients, for their effects are sometimes profound.

I wish we all could continue learning at the rate my young neighbors seem to be moving. I wish the whole Christian family could receive influence from Christians with backgrounds other than their own. I think living in the world as a Christian means listening to people and communities of the faithful that differ, as well as to those that are similar.

Take the Christians in Zaire, for example. When we were living there, we learned that faith can be vibrant without all the organizational and fiscal support we normally assume is necessary. A schoolteacher we respected had decided to stay in the village where he was desperately needed instead of moving to the city where life would be easier. He had chosen—he kept choosing—in behalf of service in a school where few books, little paper, and no external incentives for students existed. He and many other Christians worshiped in a church with no organ, no bulletins, no newsletter, no hymnbooks, and no communion sets.

When that man opened the scriptures, we learned quickly! With his teaching, the Bible seemed clearer, more helpful, more nourishing for us. Since our experiences in Zaire I have been rather critical of my own comfortable situation. I wonder if the "necessities" we Americans enjoy are not luxuries that inhibit our discipleship and stunt our participation in Christian growth. In learning, we see how much more there is to learn. Ethicists say we do change. Most say we grow in decision making as we mature. This chapter explores briefly some of those things ethicists consider important in the process.

## Do We Develop in Stages?

One scholar, Jean Piaget, studied the development of children and discovered special differences in the worlds of the very young. Children think first in terms of organizing their own physical activity. Then they think in terms of themselves, sometimes confusing their own perspectives with those of other people around them (or even with objects). Gradually, children develop more of a system of thinking, one in which they relate themselves to their surroundings. Finally, they come to think also in abstract and logical terms.

Piaget argued that these stages are natural and universal for human beings—that one way of thinking is built upon another. Pressures to adapt help force a human being to grow in ways of perceiving the world, though innate biological resources are also involved.

As part of his work, Piaget studied the moral judgment of the child. He concluded that children move from a stage of moral realism to one of autonomy. At first, in their period of moral realism, they perceive rules to exist in the world and treat those rules as powerful in themselves. Gradually, young people come to see that human beings are responsible for judging the intentions, consequences, and rules that regulate much of life. Such a view means that people can choose to cooperate and to respect good rules. It also means people can work to change rules that are not so good, to try to make better ones.

Such a developmental theory makes good sense to most of us. I remember standing under an awning with our son when he was three years old. We both watched the rain.

"Where does the rain come from?" I asked.

He pointed to the sidewalk in front of us. "See," he said, "it starts there and jumps up."

From where we stood we could not see the rain falling, nor did it hit us on our heads. He concluded the "jump" extended from its beginning in the pool of water.

Again, I listen to the children playing in the neighborhood, and one will tell another, "Don't go out of the sandpile!" The voice sounds just like that of a parent. If I ask "Why?" the child may well respond, "Just because!" or "Mom said so!" or something similar. The authority comes from outside. Yet when we grown-ups see a child leave the sandpile, our first thought is usually about the intention or the consequences of such an action, not the "rules." Is the child headed for the street? Is there another child on a nearby swing that might injure the one roaming?

Yes, children do seem to think differently about moral decisions, as they do about lots of other things. But do we human beings have to move from stage to stage in our growth? Is one way of thinking built upon another? May we not simply employ more skills and experience as we move through life? Don't grown-ups sometimes seem profoundly influenced by outside authority? Those questions are worth considering, and they have produced a great deal of debate among ethicists and teachers.

According to Piaget, the movement from stage to stage comes naturally in children, but critics ask about children with handicaps, who do not develop as most others do. And why do some children seem to move more quickly than others to another stage in moral thinking?

## Do Adults Move Through "Moral Stages"?

One researcher, Lawrence Kohlberg, who interviewed children and adults over almost two decades, found a more complex, life-long pattern of developing ethical "levels." Specifically, Kohlberg said he discovered six stages in ethical thinking. He claimed they exist as three levels, with two stages per level. As with Piaget, Kohlberg found the first stages among young children: stage one, (termed "state" by Kohlberg because it is original with human beings), in which the person responds to physical consequences of action, seeking to avoid punishment; and stage two, in which the growing person seeks to satisfy his or her own needs and is sometimes willing to do the same for others in return. Older children also generally develop to a third stage, in which they seek to please others by being "nice" and "good," according to social conventions in that society. Some move to think in a fourth stage, in which the doing of duty to maintain society is very important.

Kohlberg said some people, mostly as adults, move into a fifth stage, in which conventions and laws of society are seen as relative in nature. Individual rights, legal structures, and so forth must exist with norms of behavior for all. In addition, some few people develop a sixth stage of moral thought in which their own consciences are in accord with universal ethical principles—an ab-

stract sense of justice, a primary concern for all human rights, and
a respect for the dignity of everyone.
  These six stages can be characterized as follows:

  I. Pre-conventional level: Responsive to "good" and "bad,"
     but in terms of physical reward and punishment
     State 1: ". . . or you will be punished"
     Stage 2: "You scratch my back . . ."
  II. Conventional level: Loyal to family and social order, as
     valuable in their own right
     Stage 3: "Good boy—nice girl"
     Stage 4: "Law and order . . ."
  III. Post-conventional level: More autonomous, universal, and
     relative in thinking
     Stage 5: "In order to form a more perfect Union, establish
        Justice . . ."
     Stage 6: "Do unto others as you would have them . . ."

The scheme is a complex one. In order to illustrate its use, let's
consider briefly the different ways Tom White might be thinking
at the time of the Branford Shanty case. In each stage, he would
be in a dilemma, but his reasoning would be quite different at each
stage, as would his alternatives for action. In state one, White
would primarily fear punishment. In stage two, he would be concerned for his own welfare. At both these stages in level one,
however, Tom White probably would be a curious bystander rather
than a participant. His dilemmas would be in avoiding conflict.

In stage three White might be protesting apartheid primarily
because his friends approved of such behavior. In stage four, he
might be there because the church said apartheid is sinful. At this
stage, Kohlberg points to both A and B ways of thinking. Four A
would regard as more important the law as it exists. In this case,
White would probably be thinking "Four B"—realizing a basic
moral law had precedence over a local human law against blocking
entrances to buildings. In either case, White's dilemma would have
to do with trying to follow the law as some kind of given.

In stage five, White would be exercising autonomy in judgment,
making up his own mind about right and wrong. He would be
wanting—perhaps expecting—that the university, the transnational companies, the American government, even the South African government, create better working and legal structures for the

black majority in that nation. His dilemma would be in the weighing of influences and strategies to accomplish the task.

In stage six, White would be an exception, as was Martin Luther King, Jr., and Mohandas K. Gandhi, in thinking of more abstract principles while also attuned to justice and universal human needs. His dilemma would be more mystical and spiritual, since his sensibilities were attuned to the wider realities.

According to Kohlberg's theory, White could take the same action at several different stages in moral development. His situation makes his being at some stages more plausible than being at others.

Critics of a stage theory of moral development argue that other things are much more important than the logic and abstraction with which a person confronts ethical decisions. They say that imagination and creative responses are not really valued in Kohlberg's theory. And they say that the idea of stages really subverts the efforts of Christians to improve in their discipleship and witness.

Some critics point to the doctrine of original sin, which means that all human perceptions of reality are skewed. Stage theory does not account for the ways in which we rationalize sinful decisions in logic just as we reason through to courageous decisions. It is the kind of decisions we make that needs attention, they argue, not the ways we think about doing things.

## Does Gender Make a Difference?

At least some who study moral development believe girls and boys, women and men, differ in their ethical thinking. Carol Gilligan, among others, says that women think more in terms of relationships and of human caring. Mature men think more in terms of fairness and justice, abstractly conceived. "Morality is seen by these women as arising from the experience of connection and conceived as a problem of inclusion rather than one of balancing claims" (*In a Different Voice*, p. 160).

Notice that Piaget and Kohlberg both value autonomy more than relationships in their developmental systems. From the perspective of Kohlberg, for example, a woman making ethical judgments on the basis of human relationships—love or friendship of someone close to her—would be seen in stage three. A man deciding on the principle of justice and the attempt to treat people fairly

would be judged working on a "higher level," say at stage five or
even six.

The point Gilligan and others make is that women develop
ethical sensibilities in a different but not inferior way. As they
mature they come to consider different things important. The use
of logic and abstract principles in making ethical judgments might
be good indeed. But those tools are not better than deciding on the
basis of loyalty and love among friends. It is not less mature for
a woman to say she works in peacemaking because of her care for
her grandchildren than it is for a man to say he works in the same
cause because nuclear encounter will lead inevitably to human
annihilation.

To follow the Branford Shanty case one more time, were Gilligan to interview Tom and Jenny White, she might find Jenny
White expressing more concern about the issue of apartheid because of her friendship with the man from Soweto or her care for
the black schoolchildren in South Africa. Gilligan might find Tom
White talking more in terms of the injustice of white minority rule
by oppressive force. Gilligan's interviews might show the couple
differing in their ethical reasoning, but Tom would not necessarily
be more mature than Jenny in addressing the issue.

I wonder if men and women differ as much as Gilligan and
others say they do. Do men and women differ by gender more than
they differ as individuals within one gender? Do the ways you look
at ethical issues differ from the ways in which you find other
members of your family or your friends considering those same
issues?

## What About "Stages in Life"?

A number of thoughtful people have offered theories in recent
years about life cycles. I remember about ten years ago discussing
the work of Gail Sheehy, *Passages*. And then it was *The Seasons
of a Man's Life* by Daniel Levinson and some of his colleagues.
Both books told about adulthood in the United States, especially
about mid-life transitions for American women and men.

The values, the ways of dealing with ethical matters, changed
during those passages for both sexes. In personal and family life,
many of the people interviewed underwent crises—alienation from
a spouse, for example—or came to new determinations regarding
relationships with children or vocations. In the wider world, mid-

dle age sometimes provoked a withdrawal from deep involvement in issues of work or political life. But other people seemed to gain new meaning in trying to reform society or improve the company for which they worked. In the words of one person quoted by Sheehy, "I find I'm telling the truth more often" (p. 349). Levinson points out that people today have unique opportunities. "We have a chance to reorder our priorities," he claims (p. 338). "It remains to be seen whether we shall give higher priority to enhancing the meaning of work and to creating work organizations that foster development as well as productive efficiency."

Erik Erikson, whose study of the human life cycle provided much of the theory for both Sheehy and Levinson, emphasized the need for each person to resolve crises in order to grow fully. If the infant does not come to know basic elements of trust, for example, that person will have a difficult (if not impossible) time feeling hope throughout life. It does not mean the person is devoid of hope, but rather that in the person hope is "at risk" and difficult to sustain.

By the same token, according to Erikson in *Identity and the Life Cycle* (p. 133), if a mature adult cannot move through self-absorbing concerns, that person cannot become fully caring about others. And only the older human beings who can move through a crisis of despair to achieve "integrity," an assurance that life a. a whole makes sense, will gain the fullest wisdom possible, will be able to have "detached concern with life itself, in the face of death itself."

## Other Factors in Decision Making

While we look at factors such as gender, stage in life, and moral development, it is important to remember some of the traditional ones in ethics, such as race and class. As I have already mentioned, racial designation in America can be rather artificial, but it does influence Christians. Discrimination and prejudice have been part of American life. Sad to say, they still exercise much power in our society. As the social situation of women and men can differ, so can the situations of people in America called "white," "black," "Hispanic," "Asian," or "Native American." Among the so-called "races," there are active traditions and expectations that can vary immensely.

By the same token, class distinctions in the United States blur today (as perhaps they have historically). Yet people do "belong"—to groups and neighborhoods, social sets, country clubs, unions, and many other human arrangements based on economics and family history.

Race and class play active roles in decisions we make. When our environment at home, work, and church is similar, we are tempted to ignore these important considerations. We tend to treat all people as thinking in similar fashion, because those around us generally are. Our sense of time, our comfort in reading things, the space we "need," our love of big buildings or open fields all come in part from social conventions, affected by race and class as well as other factors.

On the one hand, considering all these factors can bring on a kind of "paralysis by analysis" in ethics. We cannot act until all the factors are known, all information sorted. Well, of course, it never fully happens and we never act. Rather, our inactivity is our decision by default in situations calling for other responses. On the other hand, considering important factors in our Christian decisions can also help us to wise and courageous actions. Moreover, the study of such factors and our consciousness of them can lead us to an intuitive consideration of them at times of crisis.

# PART TWO

# The Cases

# 5

# Decisions in Personal and Family Life

## "THIS HOUSE IS A MESS!"

"Oh, I don't know what to do. This house is a mess. I'm so scared about a break-in." Mom Breel slumped perceptibly in her chair. "I know you and Theo love me, but I feel sometimes like nobody does. It's been so hard since Andrew died. I know you're both busy, and the girls too. Maybe the Westminster Home will be the best. I'm just too tired. Thanks for coming over, honey. Don't tell Theo I'm so scared."

With mixed feelings Alice Breel heard her mother-in-law. On the one hand she realized how much Theo's mother really needed them now. She would become even more dependent in the months and years to come. It was hard to realize Mom was 84! She and Andrew, who died six years ago, had been real parents, supportive and generous to Theo and to her. But on the other hand, Mom Breel seemed to be failing in exactly the wrong ways. She was becoming more and more demanding, more full of games, and more difficult as time went by.

This situation was a perfect example. Two weeks ago, after much hesitation, Theo had gone to his mother, determined to ask her to choose either to live with them or to go to a retirement home. Mom Breel had called twice during the month before that and told them a prowler was at the house. Both times Theo had gone and found nothing. She had asked if she could stay with them for the remainders of both nights. Other complaints and worries had consumed four evenings that month—a special trip when medicine ran out, a quarrel with a neighbor, a trip to the funeral home to see the family of a church member (due to a last-minute change of Mom's mind), and so on.

Theo had gone ready to ask her to choose. But his mother had seemed so adamant about staying at her home, Theo only asked obliquely.

"No," Mom Breel had responded, "Andrew and I lived here forty-seven years before his death, and I'm not about to leave this beautiful home. Not for anything!" She had assured Theo, by his account, that she enjoyed the house. It didn't bother her that some repairs would be coming up. She appreciated the care of all her family, but she was determined to stay in the house, and that was that.

Thursday a week ago the girls had both gone to see Grandma. Betsy at 18 and Joan at 16 were awfully good about that. They reported after their visit that Mom Breel was fine. Then she and Theo had visited on Sunday after church. Mom Breel didn't go to her church very often anymore. "It reminds me too much of Andrew," she said. Theo had offered to take them all out for dinner, but she had said just a visit would be better. Alice and Theo rather enjoyed the car ride, about twenty-two miles round trip. Mom had seemed OK, talked about her friends and TV programs.

Driving home, Theo had joked that Mom Breel would "outlive us all," and they both had remarked on what seemed a good decision—to leave Mom alone about moving. After all, their house on the outskirts of town would remove her from her friends. They did have a nice spare bedroom, but it made little sense to take Mom out of familiar surroundings, eleven miles away, and disrupt all four of them. And the Westminster Home, as well as other retirement homes, would really make Mom feel like a fish on dry land.

During the week, regular visits elicited good reports as before. Then Alice got the call that produced this visit—a midday ring. When Alice answered, she could not at first understand the sobbing, incoherent person calling. Finally she had determined it was her mother-in-law.

"Mom, what's the matter?" Alice had asked.

"I'm worried. There's somebody here. In the house," Mom Breel had managed to say.

After trying to call Theo, Alice had gone over to Mom's immediately. She had patiently looked in each closet, under the beds, in the garage, and behind the workshop shed.

"Would you like a cup of tea?" Mom seemed better when Alice returned from her search. Alice agreed and listened as Mom poured out her distress. As the older woman talked, Alice thought about the future.

What a shame! A woman as interested in the world as Mom had been really was closing down. Age didn't have to be that way. Alice knew older folks whose interests seemed to broaden as time went by! Why, one of Mom's friends had really begun to travel at the age of 75!

The games bothered Alice as much as anything. Mom wanted her to tell this person something, tell that person nothing. "Don't tell Theo" was just part of the formula.

Yet Mom's physical health seemed basically intact. Sure, she had some cataract growth, a bit of arthritis, a spell of high blood pressure now and then. All seemed under control for the most part, though.

And as Alice looked around the house, she did sympathize. Both she and Theo had said, "Lord, let us stay independent like Mom." With both her parents dead already, Alice Breel, 45, wondered what to do about her mother-in-law.

Theo would have to be told, but how? He was 49. Would it be even harder on him than it seemed to her? Alice Breel considered the possibilities.

### Discussion Notes

Discussions of this case frequently yield stories from people about their own parents or other relatives in need of care. It seems more important to offer people opportunities to share personal accounts than to make it through the regular case discussion.

People naturally have a tough time gaining distance for decisions when loved ones are involved in those decisions. Yet distance—perspective—seems absolutely necessary if people are planning for times to come. On the other hand, prayer, discussion among those involved, and intimate trust are also necessary. Frequently people are reduced to playing games in dealing with matters of aging rather than really expressing their thoughts and sentiments. How are we to balance care and wisdom? What resources are there for families in times of such passages?

Discussion of this case will open other, related issues: the rights of the old, the changes in attitudes toward old people, health issues, and more. Here are a few books that are helpful.

For people like Theo and Alice, Andrew and Judy Lester have written *Understanding Aging Parents* (Philadelphia: Westminster Press, 1980). It has especially good chapters on "Changes in Our Parents' Mental Processes" and "Where Shall They Live?" Another good book is Elsie M. Pinkston and Nathan L. Linsk's *Care of the Elderly: A Family Approach* (New York: Pergamon Press, 1984).

Barbara Silverstone and Helen Hyman's *You and Your Aging Parent* (New York: Pantheon Books, 1982) has more technical data and reads like an encyclopedia, too.

Henri J. Nouwen and Walter J. Gaffney collaborated to bring photos and profound texts together in *Aging: The Fulfillment of Life* (Garden City, N.Y.: Doubleday & Co., 1974). The book helps us appreciate the beauty and needs of older people.

*Maggie Kuhn on Aging,* edited by Dieter Hessel (Philadelphia: Westminster Press, 1977), offers insights from a dialogue held several years ago, especially from Ms. Kuhn.

Some excellent studies tell about the special situations for older Americans who belong to ethnic minorities. One is Percil Stanford, *The Elder Black* (San Diego, Calif.: Campanile Press, 1978). Others in the series deal with Hispanics, Asians, and Native Americans.

Seward Hiltner, editor, *Toward a Theology of Aging: A Special Issue of Pastoral Psychology* (New York: Human Sciences Press, 1975), offers several fine articles, especially one by Paul Pruyser of the Menninger Foundation on losses and gains among the old.

Arthur H. Becker, *Ministry with Older Persons: A Guide for Clergy and Congregations* (Minneapolis: Augsburg Publishing House, 1986); James B. Boskey et al., *Teaching About Aging: Religion and Advocacy Perspectives* (Washington, D.C.: University Press of America, 1982); and Andrew J. Dobelstein and Ann B. Johnson, *Serving Older Adults: Policy, Programs, and Professional Activities* (Englewood Cliffs, N.J.: Prentice-Hall, 1985) are also useful. And a poignant passage of scripture is Psalm 31, though many other passages can also be useful in thinking about aging.

## SECOND HOME

"This would make a gorgeous place to spend vacations now, and it won't be too long before we could retire here." Don Williams eyed the pelican, which stared right back. "I wonder, though, if it's a responsible thing to do. After all, lots of folks don't even have one such house."

· Shirley, Don's wife, adjusted her floppy hat. "It makes sense economically, but we're *critics* of a gospel of abundance, not adherents!"

Don remembered what the agent had said: "Only three of these town houses left. Then all we'll have are the high-rises." He also remembered that troubling parable about the fellow who built the extra barn. He wondered if Cinnamon Caper condominium represented an opportunity or a temptation. He smiled at Shirley and waved back to a fellow waving from the deck of a small cruiser leaving a nearby boat slip.

### The Williamses

Don and Shirley Williams, ages 46 and 44, came from a large northern city. They owned a home there, where both worked and participated in church and community life. With children well along in college, however, and with every prospect of salaries increasing over time rather than diminishing, they were seriously considering the purchase of another piece of property near Sanibel Island in southwestern Florida.

Don, from a family of teachers, had moved into school administration. First as counselor, then as assistant principal, he had become one of the few principals in the system with no background as a football or basketball coach. In irony, school friends nicknamed him "Coach."

Don Williams loved his work. He thought he really contributed to the lives of hundreds of youngsters through focusing the resources of a school on their education. Northside High, by all accounts, had become one of the very best in the state since Don's arrival.

Williams also served as a member of the session, a sometime Sunday school teacher, and general participant in Northside Church. For two years he had helped in the stewardship efforts of the congregation, trying to interpret for members their wider involvement in mission through their giving.

Shirley Williams, a nurse by training, had become a supervisor and administrator in the hospital and nursing home complex not far from their house. She also served faithfully in community leadership, focusing more on voluntary nonprofit organizations such as the spouse-abuse center and the YWCA, where many programs helped women in the city.

Shirley and Don had taken seriously their responsibilities as parents. Their children—Sally and Don, Jr.—received a lot of attention and support at home. Sally, a good student and proficient flutist, had chosen to enroll at a nearby college, where she could study both music and social studies. Don, Jr., a college sophomore, had yet to declare a major. He really enjoyed the whole range of the liberal arts, and economics as well.

Frugal as a family, the Williamses had provided well for their needs in the midst of American abundance. They chose to pay cash for automobiles, even though they learned credit might enable them to receive a greater yield in interest from the investment of the money. They paid Sally and young Don's college expenses, realizing others had greater needs, even though the children might qualify for low-interest loans. Their combined incomes, including investment receipts, allowed them to save money even with double tuition and board costs. Hence their accountant urged them to locate some tax-reducing property. That conversation, a vivid memory at the end of the year, accompanied them as an "adviser" of sorts when they vacationed in the Fort Myers area.

"I'm not talking about a tax dodge," the CPA had declared. "Just find a rental property that will grow in value, obtain it with a mortgage, and watch it cost you little or nothing to own."

## "Ding" Darling and Cinnamon Caper

Don and Shirley had invited the children to join them on the trip, but both Sally and Don, Jr., said they had other plans. Don and Shirley had rented the condominium through a friend, who raved about the setup and the opportunity for investment. On arrival, they had lounged around the club pool for a while. Then they headed out to visit a local wildlife habitat on Sanibel called the J. N. "Ding" Darling Refuge. There they marveled at the birds—cormorants fishing, roseate spoonbills pruning their feathers, and anhingas (snakebirds) drying themselves in the sun. They laughed at the pelicans, admired the red-shouldered hawks, and waited quietly to glimpse the osprey. Why, they even saw a couple of alligators plying the murky waters on the edge of the preserve!

Back at the apartment, a two-story town house with all types of conveniences, they resolved to return on bicycles to "Ding" Darling the next day. The views were even more breathtaking at a slower clip, and moorhens captivated the Williamses with their bobbing and chatter. They ate at a tasty seafoood place and returned to their rented condo before the snarl of afternoon traffic.

Don took the car to see surrounding houses and apartments. He even looked at some permanently located double trailers for sale. Trailers ran from $20,000 to $40,000, condos from $40,000 to $150,000, and good houses from $45,000 to more than $200,000. Important considerations included lot size, amenities, available clubs for swimming and boating, boat slips, and proximity to the beach. Shirley saw housing on Sanibel the next day, while Don hiked to a fishing pier with tackle and bait. Shirley discovered that houses on the island cost much more than those on the mainland, and she returned to the apartment convinced that their own rental property offered as good a bargain as any. She discussed her conclusions with Don on his return. "Didn't catch anything, but I loved watching the pelicans and the sand crabs," he told her.

"Yes, we still have two town houses at pre-construction prices," the salesman confided. "They now cost eighty-seven five. We also have one for resale at eighty-six thousand dollars. Maintenance fees are three hundred dollars a month and will not go up for two years. You are welcome to pay fifteen percent down and the rest at no more than prime rate. You do need to hurry, though, for as you can tell, all but two of the hundred and twenty-five are gone. Soon we'll have only the high-rise apartments, with additional cost for boat slips, and those will cost at least as much for less square footage."

## Discussion Notes

The question of buying a second home may seem to many Christians simply a question of economics. To most, it will be a hypothetical exercise, for they cannot buy even one home of the sort the Williamses take for granted in the city where they live. Among Presbyterians, what is the socioeconomic situation? In many cases, changes in the tax law have raised pointed questions about investments.

What are Christian responsibilities regarding the building of assets? What are the major issues confronting the Williamses?

One lay leader who has addressed the topic, William Diehl, says that discussion of many issues can take place among Christians who care about doing right. In his words,

> Our society is so fantastically complex today that it is very difficult to decide what is the most just, most loving position to take on many ethical issues. We need all the help we can get to make certain we are being honest with ourselves and to see how our Christian faith applies. Every layperson who wants to relate his faith to everyday life should have access to a Christian support group, I am convinced. (*Christianity and Real Life* [Philadelphia: Fortress Press, 1976], pp. 78–79)

Remembering the biblical images and the focus on stages in moral development can help in discussion if you choose to apply them.

## GLOBAL-VILLAGE LIVING

"Look, Daddy, here's a used Datsun for eleven hundred and fifty dollars." Susan Weiss circled the advertisement and flopped the paper down on the breakfast table. "Should I call the number?"

Susan had begun some weeks earlier to review the morning classifieds with some determination, almost compulsively. With her sixteenth birthday only three months away, she relished the prospect of driving—frequently. Jeanne and Dalton Weiss, Susan's parents, shared a glance with one another, a look that meant, We'd better talk quickly about this.

"Hey, Sue, give me the funny paper, please." Jimmy deftly changed the subject, as a nine-year-old brother could do.

"Postponed a little," Dalton Weiss mused. "But the problem won't go away. It's a difficult decision coming. How can we keep all our promises at the same time?"

Dalton Weiss, and Jeanne too, looked upon decisions such as this one—whether or not to buy a second car for the family—as moral issues. Did the family have the right to use as much petroleum, steel, air, and other resources as it took to provide and operate two vehicles? Likewise, did they have a right to provide their daughter with less mobility and fewer opportunities for socialization than her friends experienced, and in other ways deprive Susan (later it would be Jimmy)? Dalton and Jeanne Weiss sensed a commitment both to the children they brought into the world and to people in the world whose needs were great.

They had not always viewed such decisions as being moral issues. Just seven years ago, they would have asked primarily the simple question: "Can we afford another car?" The answer to that query now was surely, "Yes." Dalton worked in middle management with a nationally prominent importer and distributor of electronic components. Jeanne had just begun part-time work at the church. It would not be long before she would be working full-time also. Together they certainly possessed the funds for an inexpensive second car, one Susan could use.

In fact, it worked a bit of a hardship, especially in hot weather, for them to own just one car right now. Bikes sufficed for Dalton to ride to his nearby work and for Jimmy to ride to elementary school. Susan had been riding the bus to her classes at Central High. That left the car with Jeanne almost all the time, and she could run most of the errands and drive to church for her work there.

"Just seven years ago. . . ." Dalton remembered their real turning point in thinking about the ethics of consumption. They had sold or given away almost all their possessions before serving as short-term missionaries in Ghana. Jeanne had commented at the time on the symbolic value of reducing Christmas tree ornaments to the essentials—a star, a few bright tree balls, and a small crèche, which fit in one little box. Altogether they had taken only nine barrels of things, including the needs for Jim, who had been 2, and the "little girl" needs of Susan, then 8.

The Methodist Church had advertised for someone to assist in the establishment of a new management system for the church in Ghana. In addition, they wanted an educational missionary to teach English and geography. Dalton and Jeanne decided to go. It made sense to them.

Some friends in the church where they were members had been very supportive. But many friends from the company said they thought the Weisses were crazy. Tim Adams, also at the plant, had told Dalton in straight terms, "You're thirty-one now. You'll be thirty-four when you get back. That's precisely the time span in which we're picked for eventually taking top-level jobs. You'll miss out."

Dalton remembered his and Jeanne's doubts about going, along with their joy and sense of release. The company gave Dalton a leave of absence.

"It certainly gave us a new perspective, selling the car and almost everything else," Jeanne had told folk since then. "We discovered we could live at a very simple level, even with the kids. They had fun, too. We ate well and enjoyed life, without cars, TVs, or movies. Our house was nice but plain. Working with Christians in Ghana taught us that we Americans do need to listen to others."

When the Weisses had returned to the United States, they remained conscious of world hunger and other issues that transcended national life. In Arizona, where the company had provided Dalton with a job comparable to the one he had left, they found a church deeply involved in study and work about such issues. Dalton found he could ride a bike to work, and they fell almost naturally into a simpler style of life than most families around them.

When Dalton received a promotion and a transfer to a suburb of Los Angeles, the family had looked for another Methodist church with concerned people and interest in global questions and Christian responses. Jeanne put the matter simply. "We believe that people have a responsibility to act with respect for all God's creation and with respect for one another."

The church they found was a large one, but the group within it committed to discovering ways of being ecologically responsible was small. Ten to fifteen persons gathered to study books and work on projects that might increase knowledge and commitment for themselves, the church, and the community.

They particularly enjoyed reading and talking together about the work of Ron Sider, *Rich Christians in an Age of Hunger.* They agreed with his assessment of the situation and his call for conversions to simplicity.

As their point of view led to a decision about churches, it also affected the choice of a house. Though pretty expensive in Southern California, the home they bought was in a particularly modest neighborhood. An elementary school was also near, but the middle and high schools were five miles away. Susan had been quite willing to ride the bus.

In fact, both Susan and Jimmy apparently enjoyed participating in a simpler life-style. The Weisses carefully limited their eating of meat, for example, eating mostly poultry and fish. Only occasionally did they rely on American staples—hamburger, pork chops, or steak. "Red meats are especially inefficient in using the world's resources," Dalton explained.

Limits likewise were set on the use of the television set, curtailing their exposure to advertising and to the commercialism embodied in the media. Jeanne, with family participation, set up a point system, and Jimmy and Susan could watch a lot of educational shows (at 1 point each). But they quickly ran out of points if they chose a *Dallas* segment.

"Cooperation is the key to our way of working. We try to make judgments—not to be doctrinaire, just for purity's sake," Jeanne said. "Occasionally we have squabbles, but for the most part things go very well. We are more conscious of our use of things. We also believe that our decisions affect the lives of others."

Now they faced a decision about buying a second car in a freeway society that almost took for granted the need for two cars in any family that could afford them. Susan's remark had not been a wish, just a statement of fact: "All the other kids either have their own cars or can get one almost all the time." On the other hand, cars are symbols of the worst profligacy of Americans. Would that the freeways were bike paths! Dream on. Dalton Weiss looked again at Jeanne to catch her eye.

### Discussion Notes

Can a person, a family, a congregation, or a denomination in the United States today actually live the Christian gospel? No aspect of our lives more surely contrasts with the situation in which the gospel took root than the economic. Early Christians, for the most part, were poverty-stricken. U.S. persons, at least 80 percent of us, live in comparative wealth.

Just one part of our situation can be termed the problem of communal gluttony. Our whole system depends upon profligate consumption of natural and synthetic resources. This wastefulness not only spoils the creation for us, it helps provide an economics of scarcity elsewhere. It keeps other persons in other places in need.

How to effect change? One way is by making personal and familial commitments to simpler life-styles. Many today argue that the morality of simplicity may be the only access to understanding the Christian gospel in our time.

The case presents a portion of the process as one family considers the ethics of consumption. Issues that can be foci include: family consumption, Christian ethics, depleting natural resources, conversion, and biblical authority.

Numerous books and articles pertain to this case, including Ronald J. Sider, *Rich Christians in an Age of Hunger: A Biblical Study,* 2nd rev. ed. (Downers Grove, Ill.: Inter-Varsity Press, 1984); Arthur Simon, *Bread for the World,* rev. ed. (New York: Paulist Press, 1985); and William Aiken and Hugh LaFollette, eds., *World Hunger and Moral Obligation* (Englewood Cliffs, N.J.: Prentice-Hall, 1977).

## CLARK ROBERTS AND THE PREVIOUS-LIFE READING

"Will you be my second?" Clark Roberts asked Harold Price out of the blue. Harold, who had grown up in a western state, where the term "second" applied historically to events connected with dueling, managed a simple "What?" in response.

Clark smiled, evidently a little embarrassed. "I'm going to have a previous-life reading, and I wonder if you would go along with me to record it. I'll be hypnotized, and the guy said I could have anybody there I wanted to."

"What's a previous-life reading?"

"That's when a guide takes you back over past incarnations to see what can be learned. At Omega Temple last Thursday I set up a tentative appointment, but I can change the time to suit your schedule. I also talked with a woman who had this man do one for her, and she found out all kinds of things about herself. She had been a member of the Pilgrim party that came over on the *Mayflower*. She was telling me about the experience, and this is the fellow that helped her. It'll take two or three hours one morning, and we can play tennis afterward, if you have time for both." Clark seemed very enthusiastic, both for the project and for Harold's being there.

Harold wondered how to respond. Should he work out a way to accept, or should he beg off? Should he put any conditions on his participation, or should he express to Clark once again his ambiguities concerning the whole "reincarnation" idea? He tried to sort out responses he felt and thought, to answer the invitation.

### Clark Roberts

Harold Price and Clark Roberts had been friends for two years now, since they started playing weekly tennis together at the community center. Although a few years older than Harold, Clark was clearly the superior player, and both enjoyed the exercise. As their friendship had grown, Clark had confided his interest in transcendental meditation, spiritualism, and other supernatural phenomena. He regularly practiced yoga and inquired about various doctrines and theological positions in relationship to the occult, astrology, and reincarnation. Harold, as a friend and a minister, responded truthfully as the situations presented themselves and usually enjoyed the conversations. As they talked, over lunch after games or at church before worship, Harold learned much about Clark's background and interests.

Clark Roberts, 42, had grown up working hard. He had sold newspapers as a boy, and sets of cookware to work his way through college. After working as a salesman for several firms and serving a stint in the army, he had gone to work for a paper company that supplied retail stores with a line of products. For fifteen years he had remained with the company to become a sales representative for several large clients in the Midwest. His work at present consisted chiefly in making sure outlets remained good customers, helping some new retail stores to begin operations, and doing cooperative supervision of ordering and marketing by the clients.

Happily married for almost twenty years, Clark and his wife, Grace, had three children, ages 18, 14, and 10. All the family participated consistently in the Suburban Community Church, where Harold also attended. Grace served part-time as the church hostess, and Clark had been a member of the governing board for several years.

In a previous position with the paper company in another city, Clark had been friendly with a man named Lamar Thomas, who had been interested in flying saucers, Millenarianism, and spiritual communication. He had shared this area of interest with Clark, and through him Clark had felt that some validity lay in all the extraterrestrial speculation going on. Clark had not gone with Thomas and a group of believers to await the coming of a particular saucer during that time, however. Clark described Thomas as a "dynamic person," one who "made you think about all those things."

For about a year, Clark had been attending various functions at the Omega Temple, a nondenominational "church" in the downtown area where visiting lecturers and teachers of yoga, meditation, and astrology came to speak and conduct classes. Clark had invited Harold to attend with him on occasion, especially a series of classes on reincarnation. Those Tuesday-night classes had been the subject of some conversations on and off the tennis court. What did the Bible say about reincarnation? What did it mean for God to say "I am that I am"? Had Harold dreamed or read of "previous persons" like himself?

Questions such as these had produced ambiguous feelings on Harold's part. He had responded with words. But he sometimes felt so uncomfortable that he switched the conversation to other topics, for recently Clark had begun to serve as a volunteer in a local rehabilitation program for convicts. It was an area of experience for Harold, who had previously served a year of clinical pastoral study in another setting very similar to the one in which Clark now volunteered.

## Harold Price

Harold had come to the community as a professor of church and ministry for the local seminary. Straight from graduate school and his classes in history, sociology, and cross-disciplinary studies, he had also served as pastor of two congregations in small towns. Neither previous experience nor course work had addressed the questions Clark raised: reincarnation, astrology, the efficacy of meditation, and the like. But since the subjects were sometimes in the news for their popularity, and since Harold knew of Clark's involvement in them, he began to read and to think about them.

One course in graduate sociology had reflected on Leon Festinger's *Theory of Cognitive Dissonance,* and he began by rereading the book (Palo Alto, Calif.: Stanford University Press, 1957). But even though Festinger discussed some of the items of concern in general terms, his work dealt more with decision making as a process than with any manifestation of phenomena and coping with it.

Clark also shared some of the materials he received from Omega Temple, materials Harold had never heard of before. One of the hardbound books was by Elizabeth Sand Turner, *Your Hope of Glory* (Unity School of Christianity, 1959). Presuming it representative of the various pieces of literature, Harold had read the work with some care. He found it an interpretation of the life, death, and resurrection of Jesus. In a foreword, the author said the reason for Jesus' enduring influence lay in the truth that "man is a spiritual being, made in the image and likeness of God." She separated the "meaning of Jesus" ("the man of Galilee"), from "Christ" ("the perfect self of every man"). Symbols of spiritual reality are under all the significant words in the gospels, for the author, and persons understanding this fact are helped in their spiritual journeys. Mary symbolizes "the purified soul," for example, and Bethlehem means "divine substance." "The soul (Mary), heavily charged with the divine idea, had to be unified with substance before there could be a manifestation. But 'in the inn' there is no room for the divine idea to come forth."

As Harold had read the book, he had become increasingly impressed by the idea that the author claimed absolute knowledge of the meaning of the scriptures, applied to the lives of persons today. There was none of the ambiguity, and none of the awe, pervading this way of interpreting the Bible that commonly attended his own study. Everything fit into a manageable whole—Jesus' circumcision, his "exile," his Judean ministry fit nicely into one year of time; his Galilean ministry fit into another year; his crucifixion, resurrection, and ascension. Harold recognized articulated heresies among the statements—the Docetic slant to the passion account, the Marcion dependence on only portions of the scripture, and the Arian bent of the narrative about Jesus' birth. But he had heard more scurrilous things in the name of "mainstream" biblical interpretation, and he rather liked the focus on practical usefulness of the Bible.

The author quoted throughout, as her chief and only extracanonical authority, the works of a man named Charles Fillmore, to whom she dedicated the book. Harold made a mental note of Fillmore's name and determined sometime to investigate his writings.

Personally, Harold believed in the vital truth of the Christian faith, and he really trusted Clark to be living and believing in an essentially healthy manner. Therefore he had determined not to ridicule the work or become a "big authority" on the heresies of somebody's writings. But he was interested in Clark's growth and in continuing his ministry as Clark's friend and companion in Christian pilgrimage.

Harold would not have described himself as holding to one particular system of theology. He also believed in the ultimate triumph of God's loving relationship with the world to accomplish good. As for the life and death of Jesus, Harold considered all the major atonemental theories to have expressed a portion of the truth about God's work in Jesus. He found the idea of Jesus as "example" for human beings to be the most compelling and the most believable. Pressed by questions about his convictions, he would resort to expressions such as: "I have definite hope that God will redeem the world and that the lives of those who live for good will have ultimate value in the scheme of things."

But for Harold, persons were more important than doctrines. He was fond of repeating the adage, "If God will forgive our sinful actions toward others, certainly God will overlook our mistaken conceptions about theology." Harold dismissed as "destructive" only those doctrines that deprecated some or all of the people in the world—extreme formulations of predestination used to put down other denominations, doctrines of racism, sexism, and class pride. Appealing especially were doctrines that sought to reconcile peoples and theories of existence—theologies of human liberation when inclusive, theologies of organism, and the like.

So now he tried to determine what would be most helpful, what would maintain his own priorities, and what would fit this situation. Harold knew that on several occasions when Clark had asked him to go to meetings, he had felt relieved if schedule conflicts interfered. Just why, he was not certain. But this time Clark offered a fluid calendar. Should he ask more about the coming previous-life reading? Should he ask about expectations Clark had of him? Should he simply accept the invitation and seek to learn from it?

## Discussion Notes

This case offers an entry into subjects usually ignored or even disparaged among mainline Christian congregations: reincarnation, revelation through a medium, and spiritualism. Interestingly, such subjects occupy much energy among Americans today, and many mainline Christians do also participate in séances, previous-life readings, and astrological predictions.

I have simply offered the case, asked people to describe the characters, name the alternatives for Harold Price, and then consider the theology involved.

Alternatively, you might wish to ask one participant to take the position of Clark Roberts and another to become Harold Price giving more vitality to one of the drier cases in terms of style.

# 6

# Decisions in Ministry

## THE DEATH OF FANNY GRIMES

When Rick Noble had to go into the city on business, he determined to stop and see Fanny Grimes at the hospital. She had been there off and on for the past two years. Rick wasn't comfortable about visiting in the hospital, but he supposed few people from Lynn got into town who would go by to see her. The Grimeses lived on the outskirts of Lynn, and they also stayed on the edge of the congregation. Fanny and George had always been kind of independent folk; and while Rick had known them over a long period of time, he did not see them often. The Grimeses had owned a hardware store in Lynn, and George still worked for Lonnie Beane, who bought him out five years ago. Since Fanny's illness, though, George worked only on Wednesdays and Saturdays. He was almost fully retired, probably 65 or so. Fanny must have been a couple of years younger.

After he made his business calls, Rick Noble parked and asked Information for her room number—502. Fanny looked pale, with machines and tubes, medicines, and charts around her. She still greeted him with the usual, "Rick Noble! How's the family?" Rick tried to focus on her face and pretend not to notice all the things in the room. "Fine. Gladys wanted to come with me, but I had some business to do. We're all fine. How are you feeling?"

"Oh, all right. Little dull pain here and there. They take good care of me here, though."

"Same kidney acting up?" asked Rick.

"I think it's worse than normal. They say some fluid gets around in my body and makes me feel worse than I have been. Did you see George outside?"

"No, I didn't," Rick said. "Is he staying in town?"

A nurse whisked in, apologized for the interruption, and asked

Rick to step outside a few minutes. "Is he one of your sons?" she said to Fanny.

"No, he's a friend from Lynn, a member of our church."

"I'll see you, Fanny. I'd better get on home," Rick said as he retreated toward the door.

"I wish you'd talk to George a minute if you can spare the time," she called as he backed out. "And thanks for taking the time to come by."

"I sure hope you feel better soon." Rick waved goodbye. "I'll look and see if he's outside."

George was sitting in the waiting room. Rick greeted him. "George, hi. I had to be in town anyhow, and I've been wanting to see you."

George motioned Rick to a chair. "Things aren't going so well."

"Fanny doesn't look good. All that equipment and the tubes don't help." Rick said.

"That's the dialysis machine. We have one at home. It's never even been used. I bought it for ninety-five hundred dollars just last month. It takes the fluid out of her body; they said we needed one. Then this. . . ." George's voice trailed off.

"What? It didn't work?"

"I don't know. Never got to see. I called the City Equipment Company and they won't even buy it back. No, she just took a turn for the worse, and they said she better stay here awhile. Now Dr. Knowland says the fluid has gotten in her lungs and she'll just have to stay here as long as she keeps breathing. He uses all kinds of fancy words, but it amounts to my decision. Do I take her home to die, or do I keep her here and just let her die more slowly . . . maybe next week or maybe next month?"

George lit one cigarette from another.

"If I take her home, it'll all be on me. It'll be quick and pretty sure to happen in a few days. If she stays here, the hospital will be taking care of her. She's got the pain, and it won't get any better in that department."

Rick offered George a cup of coffee. They found a little room next to the instant coffee dispenser.

"Fanny and I have been married almost thirty-five years—it'll be that on March twenty-first. These last years have really been hard ones. You know, she's been pretty sick for almost three years. Every two weeks, then every week, I had to bring her in to see Dr. Knowland. That was when things were going good. In bad times she had to stay here."

"The nurse mentioned a son. I didn't know you had children," Rick ventured. He had known the Grimeses a long time.

"Yes, Preston and Ronald . . . but they've been gone a long time now. Preston and his family live in Utah, a long piece from here Ron never married. He works for Uncle Sam. We haven't seen either one for years. Preston writes every so often, or his wife, Hazel, does. Ron just sends us something every Christmas. You know, since we've been together—Fanny and me—every Christmas has been special. We took our trips after that buying rush. Told everybody we were doing inventory. Went all the way to the Gulf coast one year. Now this. . . . What should I do? Take her on home? Leave her here?"

"What do the doctors advise, George?" Rick stole a glance at his watch.

"They won't tell me. They say it's up to me. That machine at home won't help now, though. It's never even been used! And the company won't take it back. How do you like that? If I take her home, she'll die quick. If she stays here, it won't change much. Just take longer, probably. I sure wish somebody would just come out and tell me one way or the other. What would you do if it was Gladys?"

"I don't know, George. I really don't."

"It wouldn't be so bad if there was some chance of her getting better. I don't know even if they've told her how bad it is. She acts like we'll be going home soon, like the times before. Now it won't help, though. Should I tell her?"

"George, you two have been really close for a long time. You must know best what to do."

"It's a lot on my mind. I never had to make a choice like this before. Wish I had somebody to share it with. Doctors use fancy words, but I just know it amounts to my decision. What should I do?"

### Discussion Notes

The particular poignancy of death processes in modern hospitals invites discussion and decisions of almost everyone. In this particular case, the experience has been compounded with the evident lack of a support structure for both the woman and the man. How much responsibility has the church in this situation? How should Rick Noble respond?

This case was originally offered in the early 1970s, when studies by Elisabeth Kübler-Ross first appeared in general publications. Her *On Death and Dying* (New York: Macmillan Co., 1970) still provides an excellent introduction to the issues of grief and dying, though many other good works supplement it now.

Another helpful way to study the case is to compare the reaction of Rick Noble to the various images of the Christian life presented. Will he react differently seeing himself "born again" from his reaction as a pilgrim in the faith? What if he sees himself as both?

People in discussion may well want to vent their own feelings of anger, fear, or frustration, perhaps even more than Fanny Grimes or her husband. This is a good time to listen to those words and feelings they represent.

In the late 1980s or early 1990s, technology may well have changed drastically from that shown here. You can trust the data given as truly representing the situation when the case arose. It is good to treat the situation as it is offered.

### EASTER SUNRISE

Since Gene and Ina Ross were winsome and interested, Doug
Stovall asked them to become advisers for the Centerville Presbyterian Youth Group. He explained to them that the junior and senior
high students met together, and that Gene and Ina had freedom
in the direction of youth activities. He set up a meeting with the
young people themselves, at the Rosses' request, for a discussion
of their possible service as advisers. "I know they will be de-
lighted," said Stovall, the superintendent of church school. "Several of the young people asked particularly for you, if you were
willing to come."

At the meeting, Gene and Ina presented some of their ideas: that
the young people should plan and direct their own programs for
both worship and service, that the group should be vitally involved
in all the work of the church, and that the advisers should be
resource people rather than chaperones, police, or leaders. The
young people were asked about their own responses to the Rosses
and to these ideas. Unanimously they expressed hope that the
Rosses would undertake to advise them, that they would rely on
the Rosses for resources and take charge of planning and supervision themselves, and that they really looked forward to the coming
year. Gene and Ina took the job enthusiastically.

The Rosses had not lived in Centerville very long, by small-town
standards. Fifteen months earlier, Gene had received an offer from
Centerville Furniture to head their sales department. When they
visited the town, they found that Joe Paxon, who served as president of the company, also chaired the school board. He assured Ina
that she could be hired as a teacher and asked which grade she
preferred. When she said, "Anywhere from grade two to junior
high, but I like fourth grade the best," Joe got on the phone and
in a few minutes reported, "Hey, good news. They need a fourth-
grade teacher. Why don't you go and apply this afternoon?" By the
following week, Gene and Ina were all fixed up, according to Joe,
who sent a school contract for Ina to sign along with a contract
for the house they really liked (and at their price, almost). Giving
proper notice in Warrentown and selling their house there meant
that the Rosses moved seven weeks later. Some men from the
company helped them get the new house and yard in good condi-
tion, and scarcely two months from the time of the original offer
they were well situated in Centerville. "Boy, was that easy," said
Gene to Joe, over lunch.

The Rosses found Centerville very much what they figured it would be—a typical small town, with a score of country-club families living on Moon Lake outside town, another dozen or so families of influence living closer to the business district, as did a number of small shopkeepers and middle production and sales people at Centerville Furniture, Kitchen Cabinets, Wonder Fiber, and Kiddy Clothes, the town's four plants. Most of the town's schoolteachers and leaders came from among those families. Almost all the workers in the factories and stores and on nearby farms came from the remainder of the white population. There was a small community of blacks on the edge of Centerville, mostly low-income people who served as domestics in the homes or unskilled labor around town, and several of whom were unemployed. In the words of Joe Paxon, "any Negroes with get-up-and-go have got up and went" to a larger city in a nearby county, where job and social opportunities were more abundant. Nevertheless, Joe proudly pointed to the facts that two of the long-tenured workers at Centerville Furniture were black, as was one newly hired teacher, and that black children attended the Centerville schools "just like everyone else."

The Rosses also found life in Centerville to be about what they had expected, only a little friendlier. For the most part, they worked and lived quietly and developed some close friendships. Aside from a few local eccentrics, everyone proved amiable and helpful to them. They received invitations immediately to several homes for dinner, to sail and to ski on Moon Lake, and to attend cocktail parties and other goings-on. They were also invited to worship at several churches. In Warrentown they had belonged to a United Church congregation, and since there was none in Centerville they decided to shop around. They visited the Baptist, Methodist, and Lutheran churches in turn but finally decided on the Presbyterian church because many of their new friends belonged. Joe Paxon had been an elder there and now taught high school students in the church school. After joining, they grew to like the minister, Harvey Jennings, not so much for his sermons (which were often pretty dull) as for his apparent depth and wisdom in dealing with troubled people. They became fast friends with the Stovalls, Martha and Doug, with whom they played bridge. And Gene and Ina really enjoyed the Lowry family, too, and Pete, Linda, Ted, and Louise (stair-step children) soon called them "Uncle Gene" and "Aunt Ina."

Gene and Ina, in a word, found Centerville delightful. His work was not terribly taxing, yet it was challenging. Hers was sheer pleasure. Their one real disappointment was that they continued childless. Examinations and some medications had not helped. They talked of adopting children, but what with their full-time responsibilities, they decided against it. After all, she was teaching "the greatest group of children in the world," and he was helping with the Centerville sports program. The Lowry children acted like their own; Linda had even stayed with them while the rest of her family vacationed in the mountains. Then along came Doug Stovall with the invitation to lead the youth group.

The Rosses embarked on the new duties with pleasure. They invited the youth group leaders over for pizza and discussion of the year's plans. Betty Renfroe, the president, said she really wanted them to do some serious Bible study. She also hoped they could go to a retreat in the mountains the following summer. Jim Tenney, the program chairman, said they needed to learn about other ways of worshiping God, "like from the Methodists, the Lutherans, and the Catholics." Linda Lowry, the treasurer, said they should do some "fun things" so the group would not be just like school. Nobody mentioned the Easter sunrise service.

As the school year began, the group held an ice-cream social that was a great success. The Rosses had a good time themselves, but they particularly appreciated the fact that the young people had done all the planning, collected the ingredients, made the ice cream, and drawn the crowd. They made a total of $112 on the ice-cream social alone.

They also began some serious Bible study and asked Harvey Jennings to come for three weeks to get them started. He brought some commentaries, different versions of the Bible, and a concordance and did a good job of showing the young people how to look for answers to questions about the passages they did not understand. Betty's desire to study the Gospel of John got them going, and then they proceeded to the First Letter of Paul to the Corinthians.

The young people decided to plan for the spring a series of visits to other churches. Baptist, Methodist, and Lutheran congregations were in town; they would have to go to a nearby city if they wanted to visit Roman Catholic or Jewish places of worship. Jim went to work on the arrangements.

A portion of their money and lots of time went into planning Thanksgiving baskets for the needy people of Centerville. The young people, with active encouragement from the Rosses, took a total of thirty-five baskets to elderly people and those out of work. The whole church honored the youth group for this service to the community in a morning worship in late November. They even clapped—loud applause—when Mr. Jennings told what they were doing. Well over half the baskets went to black families that the social welfare worker said were in desperate need. Jim, Chris Miller (whose family owned a large dairy farm near town), and Pete Lowry took the baskets around on Thanksgiving Eve. "It was beautiful," they said. "Everybody thanked us very much."

At Christmastime, the youth group sang carols at the homes of members of the congregation who were shut-ins. Then they all went to the Rosses' for hot chocolate and doughnuts. They also sent money to some missionaries in Japan in the name of the whole congregation. In February, Jim told the officers of the group that they would be welcome at St. Timothy's Catholic Church and at B'rith Shalom Synagogue during April. He said that visits to local churches were set up too. He mentioned Mount Zion Baptist Church in the black neighborhood and wondered if that might not be fun to see, too. But the other young people argued that they already were seeing one Baptist church, and they wanted some time to continue Bible study. So they all decided that Jim had planned enough visits for them.

In late March, only three weeks from Easter Sunday, Mr. Jennings called Gene. He said that he was very embarrassed, but at the local ministerial meeting someone had asked how plans for the Easter sunrise service were going, and it dawned on him that he had previously accepted responsibility for this year's program. Each year one church's youth group took charge, and he wondered if this would throw a monkey wrench in any of their plans. He apologized profusely for stepping out of line to speak for the young people and asked Gene to see what he could do about it. Gene assured him that the young people would help out, and he called an emergency meeting of the officers to make plans for the event.

The young people said yes, they had known about the Easter sunrise responsibility being passed around the churches, but they did not know it was their turn to take charge. Anyhow, that was no problem. Linda volunteered to lead a meditation on John 20, "short but sweet." Betty would read the scripture and lead the singing. Jim was asked to contact the churches for publicity. And then they talked some more about the upcoming visits and about the retreat planned for June. After the meeting, Ina said she really thought Harvey Jennings should have come to the youth group himself with his goof. Gene should have refused to take responsibility, since they had operated all year on the basis of youth initiative. Gene agreed with her but professed relief that it was all taken care of so easily. "Weren't the kids great?"

A few days later, Evelyn Swanson, the school's only black teacher, came to Ina's room after school. Ina had consciously tried to befriend her during the now-almost-two-years since both had started teaching at Centerville, and she assumed Eve just wanted to talk.

"It's about time!" Eve said, half laughing and half skeptical.

"For what?" answered Ina, picking up the double side of Eve's expression.

"White folks gwine let us in." Eve mimicked a Deep South patois.

"In what?"

"Don't you know? In the Easter sunrise service. Jim Tenney was by to see Reverend Anderson yesterday, inviting us to come in a couple of weeks. He didn't say much, didn't ask us to help plan or anything like that. Our minister called me because he wasn't sure how to respond. I told him that if they just wanted color in the crowd, they could bring quilts. Mr. Anderson mentioned your name, said Jim said you are an adviser for the group. He asked me to see you, to find out if anybody is serious."

"Why, I don't know much about it," said Ina. "You know, we didn't go to the service last year. I would naturally assume your church was one of those alternating responsibility. That's evidently how it's done—one youth group does it each year in turn—isn't that right?"

"Well, Ina," Eve replied, "I really don't know much about the sunrise service either, because black people have never been invited. And I understand from Mr. Anderson that there is a Holiness Church of poor whites that doesn't ever get an invite either."

"Goodness," Ina said. "I'll find out about it and let you know. That's just a sign of our ignorance. I'm sure it will work out."

"I thought you would be able to clear it up. If they really want to involve us, I think that would be fine. But if it's just another silly game, well, those days are over."

Ina thought about calling Gene at the office. Then she told herself, "That's just what we decided not to do." She waited until that night and called Jim.

"Hi, Mrs. Ross," he said.

"Jim, Evelyn Swanson saw me today about your inviting the

Mount Zion Baptist Church to the Easter sunrise service. She said they might be interested if you are willing to involve them in planning, but that they resented being asked as a token gesture. She also told me no one had ever invited the black church before, that they never had been there."

"Hey, hold on a minute, Mrs. Ross. I didn't mean to cause you trouble. Sure, I invited them, but I didn't think about hurting their feelings. I just saw the church that day we passed out baskets, and I said to myself, 'Hey, there's another church!' So I asked them. But we really should get them in on things if they feel left out. Oh, by the way, I also asked some people at the Holiness Church on Border Road. I guess they haven't been invited before either. Do you reckon we ought to get them into planning, too?"

"Jim, I guess we had better have another meeting to decide. Can you call the others and come over tomorrow night?"

"Sure, Mrs. Ross."

That was the beginning of the calls. The next day Joe Paxon called Gene into his office through a secretary (which he had never done before). He expressed intense hope that Gene and Ina could dissuade the young people from their radical idea of undercutting the sunrise service. "It's been a beautiful thing, Gene, the high point of the year for many people here in Centerville. Now I don't know whose idea this was, but I know it wasn't from you. We've grown to admire and respect you and Ina. I'm sure you would not want to ruin this for everyone."

Gene told his boss the sequence of events as he remembered them. "No," he concluded, "it wasn't our idea. And it wasn't done very well for blacks *or* whites. But after all, they're Christians and people. I've even heard you brag on how Sam and Willie Jones are among your best craftsmen. They go to Mount Zion, don't they?"

"Look, Gene"—Joe got a little red in the face—"I don't want to argue over the merits of the Negro race. I want this thing stopped quick. Either you stop it or I will. I gave over half the money for that church, and Mr. Anderson will do what I tell him. Now you better go and find out how to stop it quick, or I'll get him to."

The Rev. Mr. Jennings called that night, just as Gene got home from work. He asked to speak to Gene when Ina answered. "Gene, hi! This is Harvey Jennings. I just called to clear up this thing about Mount Zion taking over our Easter service. I've assured several people today that nothing like that was happening. What about it?"

"Well, Harvey," said Gene, "as you asked, the kids are taking responsibility for the service, like you complimented them for doing with the Thanksgiving baskets. I understand Jim invited Mount Zion Baptist and the Holiness Church, and neither had been invited before."

"The heck with the Holiness Church. I'm worried about the Negroes."

"That's funny, Harvey. They were worried about us. They were really pretty angry that we just invited them to come, not to help plan the thing. I figured you rotated it in the ministerial association but I was wrong, according to Evelyn Swanson."

"It's not funny at all, Gene. Mr. Williams of the Holiness Church won't even let us ask Mr. Anderson to join the association. Now we've got to do something to keep from ruining this service."

"Listen, Harvey, how is it the Holiness Church never took part, if their minister is in your group?"

"Well, Gene, he isn't active at all. They did come a long time ago, before we moved the service out to Moon Lake. I guess it was too far for them. But that's beside the point."

"All I can tell you is that the young people are coming over tonight for a meeting. I'll pass along your concern. Goodbye."

About fifteen minutes before the scheduled meeting, Linda called that she couldn't come. Ina asked why, and she said something vague. Jim and Betty were there, though, on time. During the evening the phone rang several times: both sets of parents (Jim's and Betty's) and Mrs. Lowry, calling to urge the Rosses to withdraw the invitation to Mount Zion. Jim was certain that youth groups from Mount Zion Baptist and the Holiness Church should be invited to help in planning the service. Betty thought perhaps they had been too hasty in the invitation, but that they ought now stick by what had been done and make the best of it. She suggested that they pray about the alternatives, and then they would meet with the Rosses, inviting the Rev. Mr. Jennings and Doug Stovall, again the following night. Betty and Jim went home.

Ina and Gene took out the Coke glasses and their coffee cups after the young people left. "How about one more cup?" Gene asked. When they sat down in the kitchen, things were really quiet for the first time all day. "You know this thing will probably cost me my job, if we go through with it," he told Ina. Then he added, "Probably yours, too."

"Yes," Ina said. "I really can't understand the hubbub. Mount Zion is mad. Our people are mad. Goodness knows about the Holiness Church. But now we have to stick by Jim. For the first time in my life, I'm glad we don't have children. We're free of this town pretty much. We've got money in the bank. Most people can't do what we're doing without getting crucified."

"You're right, I know," said Gene. "But until now we ate this place up. Why, not long ago a guy from Arlington Furniture approached me about doing sales for them, and I laughed. Now I had better explore their offer."

"Before we go running off, Gene, let's see things through. I'm already looking forward to Easter sunrise."

### Discussion Notes

The situation of Gene and Ina Ross provokes discussions in all kinds of groups. In the mainline churches, segregation has continued in fact if not in law. Whites and blacks in worship together has remained the exception rather than the rule in the United States. Understanding the reasons for continued separation can be an important topic for discussion.

Specifically, unwillingness on the part of some whites to have black people—and even white people of some denominations—participate in joint worship services remains a major topic. Exploring it can help Christians in mainline churches learn about patterns of expectations, and good discussions might help congregations discern more about their unnamed conventions.

## THE *PSYCHOLOGY TODAY* QUESTIONNAIRE

"Walt, I don't know if we can redeem the situation, or if we just ought to stop sex education at St. Mark's." Dave Lawson paused.

Walt Simmons waited on the line to see if he had finished. Walt liked Dave a lot, but the minister sure liked to talk. Sure enough, Lawson kept going after the silence.

"Would you be willing to meet with us on staff to see what to do?"

"Sure, Dave." Walt Simmons wondered whether to try to fit the meeting in on Tuesday or whether the matter could rest until later in the week. "I do feel a little responsible for the snafu. Judy, our ninth-grader, thought the whole thing kind of funny. But I can see how others might get upset."

"Well, we're really up against it. We had calls from parents of twelve of the fourteen members of the class. We'd better decide something tomorrow. What is your Tuesday like?"

Walt Simmons looked at his calendar. He thought about the situation. He'd better break into the crowded day with another appointment.

### Walt Simmons's Perspective

Judy Simmons, Walt and Beatrice Simmons's fifteen-year-old daughter, brought the paper home from Sunday school: "A Research Questionnaire on Sex."

"Guess what we did in school today?" Judy laughed at the take-off on the song Mom and Dad sang sometimes. Walt looked at the form and said, "Oh, no!" Then Judy told them about her Sunday school class.

"Mr. Thorston gave this out and told us to complete it. He ran out of copies. Mrs. Baker didn't even get one. It took us the whole time, and lots of kids giggled. Look at this: 'In your experience, what influences your choice of a sexual partner?' And this: 'What effect does taking marijuana have on you in sexual intercourse?' "

Walt looked over Beatrice's shoulder as she read the 101 multiple-choice questions and felt a sinking feeling in his stomach. This was the very questionnaire he had mentioned to Dave Lawson, Associate Pastor for Pastoral Care at the church. Dave had asker about resources on sexuality, and Walt had mentioned this piece though he had said it should be edited. But here it was, photocop ied in all its glory.

The Simmonses had just laughed at the comic nature of the thing. In the back of his mind, though, Simmons criticized Bill Thorston, doubtless unprepared again for his teaching responsibility, for not removing the inappropriate questions. Not all seminary students were so immature. Mary Baker, who teamed with Thorston, had her act together. But conversation moved on to other topics, and Walt Simmons had thought little more of the event until Dave Lawson called him the next afternoon.

"Walt? We just had a staff meeting, and I wanted to get in touch with you. You know, in Judy's class Bill Thorston used a questionnaire from *Psychology Today*. I think it was the one you told me about. Anyhow, lots of parents are upset. I got calls from four families. John Raymond got five. And Lawrence Matthews got three. To put it gently, they were all upset!

"It seems Bill Thorston picked up on my reference to that questionnaire, the one you told me about, and just made copies at the seminary library. He says he showed it to other students at the seminary, but he did not show it to Mary Baker, his co-teacher. He only had fourteen copies, and we had that many kids Sunday, so she didn't even get to see it."

"Yes," Simmons replied. "I saw Judy's copy."

"Well," Lawson continued, "I was supervising Thorston because John Raymond, who is in charge of Christian education, had a meeting out of town. I told everyone to call Thorston himself. But we all wonder what else to do. The Taylors, the Petersons, and Mrs. Jackson say they will withdraw their children from Sunday school if we have programs like this. Mrs. Jackson said one question had to do with bestiality! Well, there was nothing about copulation with animals, but there was some pretty raw stuff there.

"You were on the planning team for this whole sex education thing," Lawson continued. "You and I both think it's important for the church to address such matters as human sexuality. What are we going to do about this? What should we do with Thorston and Baker? What about the kids?"

## Background Information

Walt and Beatrice Simmons had joined St. Mark's Church eleven years ago, when they first moved to St. Louis from Houston. Walt had finished a doctoral program in clinical psychology, and Beatrice had been in an MBA program. Judy had been 4 years old, and Normie 2. Beatrice had become an officer in an area mortgage company. Walt worked with two partners in private practice, taught a bit at the university, and tried to take seriously his responsibility as husband, father, and Christian. Beatrice, too, worked in St. Mark's when she could; she would become a member of the session next year.

St. Mark's, a congregation in a connectional church, had a distinguished history of over one hundred years' duration. Founded in 1862 by Southern sympathizers in downtown St. Louis, it had been the home of several mayors, two senators, and countless local leaders in the community. Leadership for the congregation had remained extremely stable, with third- and fourth-generation members numerous on its governing board.

The congregation prided itself on the tradition of "first-rate preaching" and called Lawrence Matthews in 1965 as chiefly a pulpit leader. Matthews had administrative skills, also, and a doctorate in Communication from NYU.

Under his leadership, St. Mark's had grown to a twelve-hundred-member congregation, and the staff was increased to include, first, John Raymond, and more recently Dave Lawson, whose specialty was Pastoral Counseling. All three ministers actively cooperated in the various tasks of ministry, however; John visited and Dave helped with the Sunday school.

As a chaplain in a nearby hospital for three years, Dave had served as Clinical Supervisor for some students at nearby St. Louis Seminary. When he took the job at St. Mark's, his contract included an obligation to experiment with parish Clinical Pastoral Education. Thus he supervised the three students who did fieldwork at St. Mark's and also four others from Third Church and Broadmore. In this capacity as supervisor he worked closely with Bill Thorston and Mary Baker, who taught the class together.

Bill Thorston was only tangentially interested in parish ministry; his first love was counseling. He came from a congregational background and frequently professed mystification at the subtleties of connectional denomination relationships. Mary Baker, on the other hand, the mother of two teenagers, was an officer in Broadmore Church who decided at age 41 to enroll in seminary.

The class they taught consisted of twenty-five ninth- and tenth-grade boys and girls. Normally seven students attended, and that group was following a seven-session sequence on sexuality offered by an ecumenical curriculum publisher. Sunday was the fifth session in the series, and Bill had originally planned to use a curriculum story for class reaction. On this Sunday, however, fourteen students were present. Bill had brought only fourteen copies of the questionnaire, so there was none for Mary, nor did he keep one.

He introduced the questionnaire, with a word about its results with readers of *Psychology Today,* and passed it out. Bill noticed some occasional twitter and giggles, and the bell rang about the time students finished answering the items.

### Discussion Notes

Education for Christians has been a delicate matter from the very beginning. When Paul warned about the feeding of younger Christians, he advised starting with "milk." In contemporary congregations, there is a lot of coming and going, and some people need "milk" while others could receive more hearty fare.

This case also points to the difficulty in asking others than members of the congregation to teach children. The seminary student received supervision, but his situation in life differed enormously from that of the class and also from that of the parents.

You may wish to focus on questions of Christian responsibility, although good discussions of this case have centered also on the church's responsibility for sex education.

Though space limitations prohibit a separate section for presentation of the subsequent action, that material is given next for your information and for possible use in discussion.

Matthews, Raymond, and Lawson decided it would be most productive to write a letter to parents of the teenagers involved, explaining how the incident had happened. They decided not to provide a general mailing to the members of the congregation or to the officers, but to produce sufficient letters to supply one to each person inquiring about the situation.

In addition to the written communication, all three staff members would be present at the Women of the Church meeting on Thursday and be available to concerned parishioners at that time and during other opportunities for discussion. They thought most of the members of the congregation would not pursue the matter further after initial responses had been made. John Raymond, teaching another youth group at the time, would give special oversight to the ninth-and-tenth-grade class for the next few weeks.

*Dear Parents,*
 *As a staff we deeply regret the incident that occurred in the Ninth and Tenth Grade Church School Class last Sunday. We*

*want you to know the events that took place and share our feelings about them with you.*

*Bill Thorston was asked to teach the class for a three-month period beginning in December. The unit of study he was to conduct is contained in the curriculum of the church approved by the Christian Education Committee and is an excellent study for that age group on the subject of sex. Bill approached Dave Lawson after the first Sunday saying that it would be helpful in selecting items for discussion if the class took some sort of inventory on their knowledge. Dave agreed and provided Bill with the questionnaire, pointing out that it included material inappropriate for that age group. It was designed for a secular adult audience, not a church youth group, but it could serve as a model for constructing an inventory using appropriate material. Bill's choice, not made known to the staff, was to use the material with no changes whatsoever. Mary Baker, who is also teaching the class, did not see the questionnaire until it was handed out on Sunday morning, and played no part in the decision to use it.*

*In our opinion, Bill's decision to use the questionnaire unchanged was educationally inappropriate for that age group. Without interpretation, it could suggest that some sexually perverted practices were normal and could introduce a great deal of anxiety into an adolescent's growing sexual identity. His use of it, then, was a gross error in judgment.*

*In light of this situation, the following steps are being taken: (1) Mr. Thorston and Mrs. Baker will no longer continue as teachers in the class as of last Sunday; (2) the new teaching team, who will begin this Sunday, are Sam Thomas and Susan Lawson, both members of Second Church; and (3) the new team will begin a new unit of study.*

*We hope you will encourage your young people to attend class this Sunday. Please be assured that our concern is the same as yours: the welfare of your children.*

*We feel strongly that the church must deal responsively with the subject of sex from the perspective of the Christian faith. We in no way condone the irresponsible manner in which it was handled last Sunday in the Ninth and Tenth Grade Class.*

*Sincerely,*
*Lawrence Matthews*
*John Raymond*
*Dave Lawson*

## DEADLINE: MARCH 14

As Ed Larson left, Carl Wilbanks kept wondering which way to move in trying to resolve the problem. He and Ed were still trying to decide on a way out of the dilemma posed by Allan Fitzpatrick's continuing at Crestview Church. Only six weeks remained before time ran out and the agreement ended. Session members party to that agreement would rightfully expect termination of the pastoral relationship at the March 14 date.

Had he, Ed, and the Committee on Ministry that Ed chaired done all in their power to work things out? Should they go ahead and make the agreement openly known, as a kind of self-protection? Could they trust the process to work? Wilbanks tried to sort out the questions and to respond to them.

A pastor for fifteen years, and now for the past eight years the Executive Presbyter for City Presbytery, Wilbanks had known no more troubling situation than that of Allan Fitzpatrick, Allan's wife, Peggy, and the Crestview Church. Early in the history of the problem, Wilbanks had chosen to work personally with Fitzpatrick and to rely on the Committee on Ministry to make formal declarations and actions regarding the questions that arose. As the problems at Crestview became increasingly poignant ones, he thanked God that Ed Larson moved in to chair the Committee on Ministry. Ed, who had been a ruling elder at First Presbyterian for more than a decade, managed the personnel division for a national oil company. A deeply committed Christian person, Ed could also balance good sense with patience and a sensibility concerning the long-range good of the church. It had taken all these gifts and more as time went by. Wilbanks himself, although he did not enjoy spending such great amounts of time on one congregation's life, nevertheless felt reasonably happy with his executive role and pretty secure personally. Sure, the Crestview Church had problems—other congregations did too—but these were more than compensated for by the satisfaction that came from working for ecumenical cooperation and what Wilbanks termed "larger causes of the church." Thus, though he felt sad about Fitzpatrick and Crestview, he did not sense himself at any time immobilized or preoccupied by seeking resolution.

Wilbanks had wondered about the skills and abilities of Fitzpatrick when Crestview first called him. However, Wilbanks himself had been rather new at his own job, and he thought perhaps Fitzpatrick was just a "sleeper" on first impression. Anyhow, it was not Wilbanks's responsibility to screen incoming ministers. Peggy Fitzpatrick, Allan's wife, had almost immediately moved to the Presbytery's Christian Education Committee, which made sense because she had previous experience as a public school teacher. Wilbanks visited Crestview from time to time and heard some "pretty fair country preaching" from Fitz. He began discounting his previous ambivalence.

Three years later, in October, however, an elder from Crestview asked for an appointment with Wilbanks. When he came to the meeting, he was accompanied by three other members of the Crestview session. "Is there any way to get Allan Fitzpatrick to leave?" they wanted to know. Wilbanks asked about the nature of the difficulties the session members felt. They recounted nothing specific, except that as pastor of a nine-hundred-member church he should have better skills in administration and better ways of dealing with the staff. They thought meetings went on for a very long time and little got done. "We just don't have confidence in his leadership," they said.

Wilbanks had channeled their inquiry to the Committee on Ministry, and when the Crestview members followed through to talk with the committee, a "listening session" was set up at Crestview one Sunday night in February. There members of the session sat at small tables with representatives of the Committee on Ministry and told about their feelings of frustration: Crestview seemed to lack direction, Fitzpatrick did little visiting and almost no solicitation of new members, the educational program was in fact managed by Peggy without clear lines of communication with the pertinent leadership, and Fitzpatrick himself tried too hard to succeed and be liked and refused to take a stand on anything.

After the listening session, the committee asked Wilbanks to confer with Fitzpatrick and to invite him to attend the nearby career development center for help. Fitzpatrick went and came back thinking he wanted to serve a smaller, less complicated parish elsewhere. Peggy Fitzpatrick did not attend the counseling service with Allan; and soon after he returned, she set up an appointment with Wilbanks "to talk things over."

Thus, in May, Peggy Fitzpatrick told Wilbanks of her frustration. "I've just begun to be a contributor to this community," she said. She enjoyed her work with the Presbytery Christian Education Committee and recently had begun full-time work with the city public school system as a Curriculum Coordinator. Their children were comparatively self-sufficient, with the oldest a freshman in college and the youngest now in seventh grade. It made little sense to Peggy that Allan now wanted to take a salary cut and move to a smaller church elsewhere. They had just bought a house and begun to get established here.

Wilbanks told Peggy Fitzpatrick that Allan was encountering some difficulty in meeting responsibilities at Crestview. "Yes, but we can work them out," she declared. Wilbanks suggested that both Allan and Peggy attend the career development center together, since Allan had gone alone previously. "Sure, if it will help," was Peggy's reply.

In September both did go for a weekend at the career counseling service. After their return, Wilbanks talked to them. Allan decided he would try to take some counseling courses at the medical center in the city, both to help him resolve his personal dilemmas and to equip him for finding work as a chaplain. If he moved into chaplaincy, there would be fewer familial expectations and they might be able to keep their house, where Peggy and the children who were still at home were happy.

No sooner had this course been set than the members of Crestview's session called again. "We have told the Committee on Ministry people, but we want to tell you too, that things are worse now at the church. Allan has fired our competent Director of Christian Education, which he did not have the right to do himself; she was responsible to the session through its Christian Education Committee. He's doing less and less here that helps." As it turned out, Allan Fitzpatrick thought he had simply told the D.C.E. to do things better, not fired her. But she considered some of his statements, such as "The next time you do so-and-so you'll be gone so fast that . . ." to be threats that made her work position untenable.

At an October meeting attended by Allan, Ed Larson, who had become chairperson of the Committee on Ministry in September, three members of the session, and Wilbanks, a tentative decision was made to seek an agreement from session whereby Fitzpatrick would have some time off for looking elsewhere, his dossier would be updated, and the offices of Presbytery would be used to urge him along in the process of relocation. The session agreed that Fitzpatrick really should look for other work, with no one dissenting strongly in the nonconfrontational atmosphere of the subsequent session meeting.

Wilbanks knew that Fitzpatrick was working to relocate. He had had calls from at least two churches during the Advent season and a couple more in the spring. Each was an initial inquiry, and he heard no more from any. Fitzpatrick himself said that he had tried to find a counseling position in the city first, but there seemed to be none available. He was following through on the courses, and Crestview members seemed to understand the situation.

In June, however, Wilbanks received a letter from Ben Richards, the Clerk of Session at Crestview. "Resolved: That Crestview Presbyterian Church seek assistance in its continuing problems of pastoral direction." At the bottom of the formal letter, Ben added in longhand, *We surely need help right away!* Wilbanks and Larson met on July 14 with session and separately with Fitzpatrick. All agreed that an eight-month period would be established during which Fitzpatrick would be paid for a final two months beginning January 14, with no other responsibilities than to preach and to seek employment elsewhere. Because they felt publicity would impair his effectiveness as both job seeker and pastor at Crestview, the agreement would be formal but confidential.

Now the two-month period had begun, with Fitzpatrick still quite unsettled. Only one congregation had responded during the fall to the dossier, a struggling church in rural Kentucky. Fitzpatrick said that Peggy did not even want him to consider it. Wilbanks had mentioned an opening for a director at the senior citizens' home and counseled Fitzpatrick to look into it. Wilbanks himself had been forced to express hesitation, however, when the search committee for that job had inquired about Fitzpatrick's administrative ability. There was an opening for an assistant chaplain at Methodist Hospital, but Wilbanks supposed better qualified persons would apply for that job.

Larson had been in for a meeting about the church the Presbytery was beginning in New Town, but both he and Wilbanks had not considered Fitzpatrick seriously for that responsibility. "He's such a lovable person," Larson had said afterward, however. "How is the search coming?"

"It's not looking good for him," Wilbanks had confided.

"Is there anything the Committee on Ministry can do right now?" Larson had wondered.

"No, nothing I can think of. We'll have to share the situation with the congregation pretty soon," was Wilbanks's parting thought.

## Discussion Notes

In the beginning session on church polity, I still remember the professor screwing up his face and announcing, "The Presbyterian system is something weird." He proceeded to introduce us to the vocabulary and rules of ordination, location, demission, and retirement (among other things). This case, which follows an actual though disguised situation, illustrates the working of the "calling system." More precisely, it illustrates problems and issues that arise when the wrong person is in the wrong place at the wrong time.

| | |
|---|---|
| Administrative | What steps can be taken to relocate pastors? |
| | Who should take steps? |
| | Where do responsibilities of administrators lie? |
| Ecclesiastical | What systemic problems are apparent? |
| | What impingements are there on the congregation? |
| Ethical | What confidences are there? |
| | How do matters of care meet matters of efficiency? |
| | Who bears responsibility? |
| Pastoral | Care for whom? |
| | Do pastoral issues conflict? |

Discussion of this case is particularly helpful within the system, but the major issues cross all denominational lines. For other communions, however, the following definitions might be helpful. You may also want to summarize the pertinent rules, as found in the *Book of Order,* Part II of the Constitution of the Presbyterian Church (U.S.A.).

**Elder** elected and ordained lay leader of a local congregation

**Session** governing body of local congregation, composed of elders with minister as moderator

**Presbytery** comparable to a district or diocese, with all ministers of the Word as members, and an equal representation of elders; functions as a "corporate bishop" in many respects

**Executive Presbyter** person (usually minister) hired by Presbytery for administrative and pastoral functions in Presbytery

**Committee on Ministry** Presbytery body charged with care of ministers and their relations with local congregations

**D.C.E.** Director of Christian Education, a member of the staff (usually of a local congregation)

# 7

# Decisions in Vocation and Political Life

## BRADLEY JOHNSON, VOLUNTEER

Working the route when he needed to think gave Bradley Johnson pleasure indeed. As a postal carrier he sometimes got bored, as would anyone else doing a routine task. But when he had to make a decision, the occupation of his hands and the rest of his body seemed to free his mind.

The problem this Saturday morning centered around LeRoy Hipps, but it extended beyond the individual to encompass the whole food distribution system. Maybe his eyes had deceived him, Johnson thought, but he could have sworn he saw Hipps exchange money for drugs. Some food had been pilfered, and Johnson himself had already suspected Hipps. What a terrible plight for the young man if Hipps had become involved in the street traffic.

Bradley Johnson rounded the corner where the cocker spaniel barked. He took out letters and a magazine for Yvette Barton and placed them in the box. Was there mail for Sam and Dottie Black? He moved quietly along 34th Street, toward Maple from Shawnee Parkway.

The deeper problem was the system. Surplus food could be distributed to the poor, nutritious food, sorely needed. But from the system agribusiness flourished, small farmers gave up, poor people became more dependent on irregular "gifts" and stood in line to compound their sense of general humiliation. Grocery chains enjoyed the system, dumping outdated stuff and claiming deductions too, he supposed. Further, the system could give occasion to young men such as LeRoy Hipps to rip off some food and find himself caught in a cycle of deception and drugs.

Johnson could talk to Hipps. As a volunteer for four years, he had earned that right. And Hipps respected him; Johnson knew that. But what could he say? What could he do? Would the conversation be taken as an accusation and cut off communications? Hipps had given real promise of maturing. Could Johnson have been mistaken?

Bradley Johnson arrived at Maple, turned toward 35th, and gathered the letters for the Miltons. His own volunteering might be contributing to the system. He loved it, mind you. Every Thursday afternoon, from 3:30 to 7:30 P.M., he helped the Fairfax Center with its regular distribution. Usually Johnson verified the names of recipients and marked their receipt of the cheese, potatoes, eggs, canned goods, or whatever. Sometimes he served walk-ins, new residents of the project or folks not yet scheduled for the regular monthly pattern.

Johnson, as a longtime resident of the neighborhood, knew most everybody, young or old. He and Viola had bought a home, fixed it up, and stayed, though some neighbors and friends sold at the time the project began. The Johnson children were away, all three living happy, involved lives. And Bradley Johnson felt he and Viola enjoyed the stability of keeping their home.

Lots of mail for the Turners, who had just started delivery again after a visit elsewhere. Just one letter, no bulk mail, for Myra Thompson. He worked his way toward his jeep, parked at 35th and Shawnee.

Hipps shared many of the burdens common to most project folks. His mother tried to cope with three children, LeRoy the oldest. Though his attendance at the center was irregular, Hipps seemed preoccupied and worried when he did come to help. He told Johnson that school was OK. He wanted to finish high school and try to make it in college somewhere.

Johnson would open their conversation with a "How're you doing?" Hipps would then talk a lot—about how his sister and brother made too much noise, about how his mother tried to sleep but worried so much, and about school things that were upsetting.

Last Thursday, the youth had disappeared more quickly than usual. No goodbyes, no waves of the hand. This Thursday, Johnson had been told about the loss of food. Not a lot had been taken: just 35 pounds of cheese and a carton of sardine tins, as far as the staff could tell.

Hipps had arrived late—about 5:30 P.M.—but that was not uncommon. Johnson noticed that the young man stayed around the closets, where the cans and other nonperishables were stored. Staff members and volunteers were watching to lock things up. Hipps left about the regular time, waving to Johnson and the rest.

Friday, yesterday, on his way home Johnson had seen the exchange, on the corner by the liquor store. It could have been anything small received by Hipps, but it was surely money that was given. Johnson didn't know the older man who took Hipps's money and gave him something in return. Alcohol for minors changed hands there, but the thing given seemed too small to be a bottle.

Johnson hoisted the sack beside him into the jeep, drove to 37th Street for the two-block walk around, and sat to sort out the next batch before starting his rounds.

## Discussion Notes

This straightforward situation, mostly personal in nature, has produced discussion also personal in content. Seldom has it moved to consideration of the structural issues also involved. I encourage discussion leaders at least to ask about the more complex structural issues—the caring institutions of American life, the temptations inherent in a society of plenty in which some people have little, the problem of drugs, and the responsibility of citizens to provide information to law enforcement officials regarding illegal activities. Many others can be named, but these were on my mind as I drafted the case itself. They were also on the mind of the person who gave me the case.

Recently in many communities the difficulty of depending on volunteers has become apparent. A number of cities now provide recognition to volunteers through awards and features in media. What are we to make of such efforts? Do they help or hurt or not essentially affect the nature of volunteering?

A friend recommended recently the works of Marlene Wilson in this area of study. I have found them especially helpful: *The Effective Management of Volunteer Programs* (Boulder, Col.: Volunteer Management Associates, 1976); *How to Mobilize Church Volunteers* (Minneapolis: Augsburg Publishing House, 1983); and *Survival Skills for Managers* (Boulder, Col.: Volunteer Management Associates, 1981).

Also helpful, although out of print, is Anne K. Stenzel and Helen M. Feeney, *Volunteer Training and Development: A Manual for Community Groups* (New York: Seabury Press, 1968).

On the issue of drugs, many resources come best from members of the class, who might be invited to bring and share materials at the time of the discussion. Some good books are William R. Miller,

*The Addictive Behaviors: Treatment of Alcoholism, Drug Abuse, Smoking, and Obesity* (New York: Pergamon Press, 1980); Oakley S. Ray, *Drugs, Society, and Human Behavior,* 3rd ed. (St. Louis: C. V. Mosby Co., 1983); Pauline Neff, *Tough Love: How Parents Can Deal with Drug Abuse* (Nashville: Abingdon Press, 1982); and Kathleen R. O'Connell, *End of the Line: Quitting Cocaine* (Philadelphia: Westminster Press, 1985).

### "YOU GET BACK WHAT YOU SOW"

"It surprised me. I just stammered." Charles Jenkins laughed at himself. "Then I told Jerry I would get back to him. Gosh, Beth, I don't know what to do."

"He had no right to ask you." Beth Jenkins could feel her anxiety level rising. What a quandary for Charles to be asked to contribute to a political fund! It might be downright illegal if the bank gave him an equivalent bonus in exchange for a contribution. State politics! Was it all like this?

Beth sympathized with her husband. She wondered how to help him in his decision. Well, actually, they would make the decision together, but Charles was the one put on the spot.

Maybe if she and he had not both come from such sheltered homes. Maybe there were ethical guidelines for such things. It did seem dirty, though, for a bank owner to ask one of his officers for such a contribution. Jerry Owens, who also owned banks in four other counties, had not actually hired Charles Jenkins; he had delegated such ordinary personnel matters to bank president Dick Withers. But Owens let everyone know that he had the final say. Now he had approached Jenkins with a definite request.

"Charles." Owens had put an arm on the shoulder of the trust officer and looked him in the eye. "Charles, I know you think highly of Bruce Samuels, who is sure to be our next governor. You know he needs help fighting Henry Peabody and Mary Ford Robbins. I know you'd like to help him. Under the law nobody can contribute more than three thousand dollars. Well, I already gave mine, and my wife Barbara's too.

"But if you could see your way clear to put in three thousand, that would be great! Even better, maybe Beth could put some in too. Anyhow, your bank is having a real good year. You won't be out any if you make a contribution. I personally guarantee it'll come back to you. Why, you'll even get a little tax deduction for your trouble. 'Cast your bread upon the waters. . . . You get back what you sow.' "

Charles Jenkins tried to show as little reaction as possible. "Well, Jerry," he had replied, "I'll have to talk it over with Beth. I'll get back to you."

Charles and Beth Jenkins had lived in Tennessee for only four short years, the time of Charles's employment at the Saylor bank. Both he and Beth had grown up in North Carolina, he in Asheville and she in the manses of various communities in which her family had lived. His parents had both taught school, while her father had been a minister. They had met in college and had married before either had received a bachelor's degree. The job in Saylor had been advertised in the college placement service:

> Honest, intelligent, loyal person needed to be trust officer
> for a small, thriving bank in Saylor, Tennessee. Business
> majors preferred. Salary negotiable.

Dick Withers, president of the bank, had done the interviewing. Withers told Jenkins that the bank owner, Jerry Owens, took a personal interest in the officers and tried to promote from within his banks and other business interests. With a child on the way, Beth and Charles had jumped at the possibility of bringing up a family in Saylor. Eliza was born five months after they moved to Saylor and Bert was born nineteen months later.

Saylor was indeed a great place to raise a family. Charles enjoyed his work at the bank. He and two other officers shared with Dick Withers in making most routine decisions. Weighty matters such as large loans and rescheduling of payments always needed an OK from Jerry Owens.

But, of course, Jerry and his family did own a majority of the bank stock.

Owens definitely had personal political ambitions, and he especially liked to hobnob with people in state government. He seemed to support and enjoy being with certain members of the majority party who called themselves the Regulars. Their candidates had won the statehouse and a working majority in the legislature for the past two decades, but the other political party had taken the last general election and elected the governor.

Neither Charles nor Beth Jenkins ever expected to hold office, but both had been attracted by the candidacy of Mary Ford Robbins, a member of a reformed wing that had recently been organized to offer a choice of candidates in the party primary. Such "Reformers" were opposed to the traditional power that the Regulars exercised. In addition, a very attractive physician, Henry Peabody, had joined the fray.

### Discussion Notes

Though not on the scale of White House arms deliveries to Iran and secret payments to the Contras, or even of insider trading scandals, this case broaches many of the same issues. The quiet circumvention of laws, if not their downright violation, becomes a problem for many people in business and government. Questions of authority and responsibility for actions and policies, problems related to hierarchy in a chain of command, and matters of truth telling or disclosure all claim attention here.

Because of the scandals of the Reagan administration and on Wall Street, articles calling for higher standards of ethical behavior, as well as those calling for the development of character on the part of leaders in state and industry, have become common in major periodicals. One excellent resource is the *Harvard Business Review* for the second half of 1986. "Why Good Managers Make Bad Ethical Choices" by Saul Gellerman (July-August issue) provoked many letters in subsequent issues of the *Review,* including an excellent one by Max Bader, M.D., of Seattle, Washington. That sequence of articles and letters addresses many aspects of business ethics, including the practice exposed here by Jerry Owens's request.

Discussion of this case may offer a good occasion for participants to share accounts of seeking to establish or enforce standards of ethical behavior where they work. It may also afford a chance for people to share their dilemmas, even to confess their shortcomings and cynicism about policies and standards. I have used the case with a group of seminary students and with a church group. Both instances provoked personal expressions from some members of the group, as well as good exposure to areas of ethics that usually are ignored in church situations.

Another excellent exchange occurred when, in discussing a different case, the question was raised, "What happens to an honest person in business today?" Almost all participants were business people, and they shared mixed opinions on the subject. Afterward, one man said he really appreciated the chance just to broach the issue in a church group and that from then on he was determined to give support and encouragement personally to friends and other members of the congregation caught in sticky situations.

The case also offers a chance to take up questions about stages in moral growth and to explore different questions about gender, development, and other factors.

## PLANNING MONDAY

### Part A

"Sandra, could you sign off soon? I need the phone," Paul Burton called to his daughter. She signaled back that she would, and Paul glanced at the calendar in front of him, trying to figure the time he needed to set aside for the funeral and for being with the Willis family. Hank Willis had died suddenly of a heart attack last Tuesday while vacationing in Florida with his wife, Mary. Now, on Sunday night, Burton was planning his Monday, with ministry to the Willis family and close friends a first priority. The funeral would be at 4:00 P.M. Burton knew he would function best if other matters did not clutter his mind.

Ideals seldom can be realized, however, even in a small town. Ministry gets hurried, even with a comparatively small congregation. "Things have a tendency to cluster." Burton remembered the wise aphorism of an older pastor. On his calendar for the next day Burton had made a note that Martin Lyles would undergo surgery in the morning at Tulsa Hospital. That was almost an hour away. And Mike Hennessey was still at General, another Tulsa hospital. Also noted were *Teen Center grant, Mrs. Graves 10:30,* and *School Board, 7:30.* Burton's first call would be to School Superintendent Riggins. He usually checked in before regular meetings. At this one, the contract of the band director would be under review, along with the consideration of hiring another person to help in school music. Should Burton beg off that meeting? As a member of the school board and as a minister to the Willis family, he wondered what he should do. And how much else could he accomplish?

Sandra clicked the phone down and patted her father on the back as she passed him on the way to her room to do homework.

### Paul Burton, Minister

Paul had majored in engineering and worked for a large oil company almost six years before deciding to enter the ministry. At first his wife, Carol, had not altogether approved of his change of

---

This case contains two parts. You have the choice of reading and discussing either one of them or both. You may wish to devote two sessions to this case, one on A and another on B. If you do that, participants should not read Part B until discussion of Part A has been completed.

vocation. Her mind changed gradually, first to acceptance and then to full support. Burton considered his theology "pretty conservative." He believed that God does answer prayers, that Christian churches are obligated to service in the world, and that the Bible remains the central authority for both ministry and life. Cheerful and dedicated to his family and his church, Burton received several opportunities for ministers upon graduation. He chose to serve a church of 280 members in a town of 11,000, about forty miles from Tulsa, Oklahoma. With anticipation of good opportunities for living, the Burtons had moved to town in the summer of 1972 with their two daughters, Marie and Sandra, ages 15 and 10. Gradually his ministry had focused on the health of the community, as well as on the spiritual growth of the congregation he served.

In 1974 Burton had agreed to run for a place on the seven-member school board, governing the town's high school and three "feeder elementaries." He won handily. On the board, he quickly recognized the need for a teen center to offer a healthy environment for after-school activities. His interest in a teen center was matched by that of some parents and other responsible grown-ups in the congregation. So the church's governing body and local community members began a nonprofit corporation to run a teen center. Burton helped locate and secure an old school building, assisted in the transfer of its title to the Teen Center Corporation at a nominal cost, and coordinated the fund drive to gain money for renovation and program. The Teen Center now received several thousand dollars and a good director of activities from the budget of the town. Dances, games like pool and Ping-Pong, some classes for arts and crafts, and a snack bar offered students and other teenagers some variety in activity and constructive recreation.

Now the Teen Center Corporation had only one month to initiate a proposal that might result in foundation money for both renovation of the building and staff to increase program. Since he had located the possible funding source through friends in Tulsa, and since his skills included "grant writing" (at least to a certain extent), Burton had been asked to formulate the proposal draft, due April 2. At one point, he had figured time for that task on March 14.

At church, Burton had found that few committees functioned, and the leadership pool was quite small when he came to town. His pastoral visits, work to enable the functioning of committees, and enlarging the numbers of reliable leaders had soon begun to show results. Attendance at church, a ready indicator of congregational life, had grown from 125 to an average of 170 for regular Sundays, and the membership to 300. The budget had more than doubled in five years. A more helpful indicator, however, was the growth in diversity among church leaders. New families had joined with a wide variety in backgrounds. One had been involved in Ecumenical Institute; another, in leadership of Young Life. Still others came with no religious background to speak of.

Burton realized that with Tulsa's growth, the health of the congregation, and the constrictions of present facilities, a new educational building should be constructed. With the permission of the board, he asked a friend in Oklahoma City to provide some preliminary ideas. In January, the concept studies for an educational wing began to circulate among members for their suggestions. Soon a plan must be formulated to undertake the fund-raising. Burton began asking around to discover the best person to lead the building fund committee.

At church, Burton had increasingly become a pastoral counselor for members—and for some nonmembers as well. He considered this function an important one and would have liked more concentrated training than his two seminary Clinical Pastoral Education courses. But he listened, kept confidences, and was willing to go to bat for people when he could.

Mrs. Graves, with her 10:30 A.M. appointment, represented a portion of that ministry. She had been racked by a divorce that left her unprepared for life without a provider. Burton had made the appointment for her before she left for a visit to her folks' home in Amarillo. She would want to talk about her kids, about her ex-husband's not paying promised alimony, and about trying to enter the job market: Should she stay in town, or should she move back to Texas? Did he still have time for the appointment, even if he could move it to later in the day? Could he get in to Tulsa for hospital visits, back out, eat, and have time to see her before the funeral?

## The Week Before

Monday, March 7, Burton had spent the first hour in prayer, Bible study, and sermon preparation. Mail and routine things had taken the rest of his morning. He had eaten lunch with some businessmen, talking in general about the needs of the Teen Center. Some counseling had been a portion of the afternoon's work, along with a trip to see shut-ins on the eastern side of town. Monday night, and a portion of Tuesday, his regular day off, Paul had spent at home.

Tuesday night Paul had talked on the phone at length with Mary Willis, comforting her and helping plan the funeral for Hank. Burton had explained that he would have to be in Dallas Friday, the day Mary originally picked for the funeral. But he could lead the service either Saturday or Monday. Mary had willingly chosen Monday, since it would give her widely scattered family more time to gather.

On Wednesday, Burton had prepared for the meeting of synod's Committee on Ministry, to which he would go Thursday and Friday. He had worked on the Bible study he led each Wednesday night, and he had outlined Sunday's worship and sermon. Wednesday night he taught the class.

Thursday morning, early, Burton had gone into Tulsa and visited Mike Hennessey before leaving for Dallas on the nine-forty flight. Friday, by phone, he had learned of Martin Lyles's projected heart surgery.

On returning Saturday, Burton again stopped briefly by Hennessey's room. His recuperation from stomach surgery was proving slower than expected, and the family wondered if the doctors were leveling with them. At home he finished the worship elements for which he was responsible and then visited with the Willis family for about an hour. At the church on Saturday, Frank Watson, the janitor, expressed some apprehension about retiring. He had only social security, and a minimum of that, to live on. Burton wondered if the church could, or should, supplement the income of this man, who had worked for them for the past twelve years, but only part-time.

Sunday, full of morning worship and another visit to the Willis home, had allowed little time for rest. Ideally, Burton would have written notes for any worship elements to be printed in the bulletin on Sunday afternoon for the next week. He still had not found a sermon, either, for March 20. An irate parent called on Sunday afternoon—her child had been expelled from high school for fighting. Carol, who answered, referred her to the school principal, but she said she expected Burton to return her call.

**"Planning Monday"**

Burton focused on the calendar. How much could he accomplish? Wherein should his priorities lie? He returned to glance at the week ahead:

Could he make the school board meeting at 7:00 P.M. with a 4:00 P.M. funeral?
Would he be able to take off on Tuesday?
Could he see both Hennessey and Lyles?
Should he keep the appointment with Mrs. Graves at 10:30 A.M.?
What guidelines, if any, could he rely upon to inform his choices?
What had he neglected to include in planning for Monday?

He began to dial the number for Superintendent Riggins.


## Part B

Tired, Paul Burton put down his red pencil and looked at his desk calendar. He still had another several pages to write. Maybe he could finish the draft in a couple of hours. Should he stop for the night and try to polish it off in the morning? Since Tuesday was his day off, should he put off drafting the rest of the proposal until Wednesday? Or should he just plug along some more?

Burton wanted to get the proposal written, at least a draft of it, to pass to friends who knew how to make it sing. The Teen Center could be helped immensely by foundation funding, if it came. But today was only two weeks before the deadline. He didn't want to put off the drafting, because Jonathan Sills at the University of Oklahoma could read "grantese" and would need time to go over it. That argued for getting it done tonight or tomorrow, Wednesday at the latest. But if he broke into his day off with too much work, would there be any time at all for recreation? Already there were at least two calls to make—possibly a visit. In Tulsa, Martin Lyles was not doing well at the hospital. And a call to the Willis home would tell if the kids were going to be in town all day. Maybe he should see them awhile before they left town.

What about the day off? Would it be gone by then? Burton doodled on his memo pad while he thought.

## Monday's Plan

Burton had arranged Monday's schedule to allow four and a half hours with the Willis family, if that much time was necessary. He would begin the morning with a visit to the two hospitals in Tulsa, calling from the city if he ran late to postpone the counseling with Mrs. Graves. He would eat a late lunch with Carol at home, then rest a bit before going to the Willis home at 3 P.M. He would offer to drive at least some of the family to the funeral home. He would go back home with them and stay as needed.

He would miss the school board meeting in order to try to write the proposal after supper, drawing as much as possible from the notes provided by the Director of Activities now employed. In conversation with Superintendent Riggins, Burton had asked what matters of importance would be coming up. Riggins had mentioned only the need for an assistant band director/music teacher.

"We really should hire someone to do it," Burton had commented. "Why, when you consider per student expense, an assistant football coach costs a lot more, and we have one of them."

"I agree," Riggins had responded. "I don't foresee any difficulty. Can I call if I need you?"

"Yes, I'll be at the Willis house or maybe back here by the time you get to that issue."

Missing the school board meeting was a bit risky because other matters could come up. But budget items had to be read at two meetings, so he could consider them later. He felt it extremely important to allow time after the funeral, not to rush to another commitment.

As for the hospital calling, Burton knew there was a possibility of very early surgery, but most times the patient was not readied until about eight thirty. While he was in Tulsa, it made sense to stop and see Mike Hennessey, evidently still depressed.

Burton felt postponing the meeting with Mrs. Graves would be possible, and better than canceling the appointment. In addition, he would probably have time to do a little of the routine planning for next Sunday's worship and the bulletin.

Burton's calendar looked like this:

| A.M. | 8:00 | Be in Tulsa, see Lyles |
| | 9:00 | General, see Hennessey |
| | 10:30 | Mrs. Graves |
| | | Get notes on Teen Center proposal |
| | | Church routine |

P.M.    1:00    Home, lunch
        3:00    Willis home
        4:00    Funeral
        7:30    Home, supper, write proposal

## Monday

Tulsa commuting traffic on Monday morning moved with surprising ease. There were interstate highways almost to the door of Tulsa Hospital, so the forty miles could be traveled in fifty minutes. Burton, who had allowed a full hour, arrived ten minutes early—at seven fifty.

It was a good thing. He had no sooner entered the room than the orderly came to take Lyles to surgery. They shared a prayer, Burton, Martin Lyles and his wife, Sara, and Mildred Hopkins, Lyles's sister who was there, too. Burton offered to buy coffee for the two women, and they talked a little in the snack shop. Sara was nervous because tests had shown Lyles's blood pressure high, and the operation itself gave a sense of foreboding to all concerned.

Traffic between Tulsa Hospital and Tulsa General was bad. Burton stopped for gas along the way. He still made it to General by five minutes after nine but had to wait outside Hennessey's room while he was being given a bath. Mrs. Hennessey was in the waiting room, and she said things were not improving. "Could it be cancer?" she asked. The doctors had said it was just diverticulitis and that Hennessey should begin to get stronger soon.

Prayer with Mr. and Mrs. Hennessey was difficult because she began to cry softly in the middle of it. Hennessey said little and seemed quite distant.

At nine forty-five Burton called the office to leave word that he was on the way to church. "Please tell Mrs. Graves just to wait." He asked about messages. "No, just Pauline Jones saying she would bring the notes over for you to write the proposal for the Teen Center."

He arrived at the church at 10:45 and talked to Ethel Graves about her plans. He could see she wished him to give advice on her decisions about the future. He did tell her about the Human Resources staff in state government and the cooperation with county court to locate and obtain child support payments from her ex-husband. He resisted telling her to either move back to Amarillo or not. At eleven forty-five he tried to close off their meeting. She wanted to set a time for another counseling session the following

Monday morning at the same time. Burton suggested they wait two weeks at least, until she could assess prospects of moving or staying and have time for some job hunting.

He opened the day's mail at noon and had just begun dictating a response to a letter from the Presbytery executive about agenda when Frank Watson came in, wanting to talk. Underneath his conversation was the question, not asked, "Have you done anything about my pension needs?" No, Burton had not yet thought about it to form a way of proceeding. He just talked awhile, and then Burton realized it was one thirty. He managed to write a prayer of confession. Hungry, he doubled his efforts and selected hymns for the secretary to check with the organist before including. Marjorie Wilkes called to say she heard that Liza Gaines was sick.

Burton called the Gaines home. Liza was not there. He took ten minutes to go over some details with the church secretary and went home: 2:00 P.M.

Carol had already eaten. She had left a note:

*Liza Gaines to go to hospital next Monday. Mr. Riggins called. I'm subbing this aft. at G.A. Sandwich in fridge.*

*Love,*
*Carol*

Burton tried again to call Liza Gaines. No answer. Riggins, too, was out, but his secretary said it was just about the disciplinary code revision, not due until May's board meeting. Burton ate the sandwich and drank a glass of milk. He studied the Bible and a guide for the series while he rested a little while. A text in Amos looked like a good sermon-in-the-making. He looked up the verses in a commentary.

At three he went to the Willis home, found them grieving in a "pretty healthy" way, met some of the children and other family, talked with them.

At four the funeral took place at the funeral home. Lots of folks were there and almost all went to the graveside services.

At five, when people were leaving the cemetery, Burton drove part of the family back home. Carol came by also, to say hello and to see if anything was needed. She had been working at Allen's law firm, as she did when Gerald Allen had to be away in court.

Burton talked and listened, mostly listened, as the Willis children told about life in their family. Burton was pleased that everyone spoke warmly of Hank Willis, a fine man. That meant they would be comforting each other openly.

He got home at six thirty, feeling a little guilty about not making the board meeting. He ate supper and relaxed with Carol and Sandra, talking about everyone's day. At seven forty-five he began to work on the proposal, the notes hand-delivered by Pauline Jones, the Program Director.

Now he had written four pages by 9 P.M. He had at least as much to go, maybe more. He would like to just stop. He wondered about waiting, though. Would he save time by just plugging along?

### Discussion Notes

The use of time is a major ethical consideration. Several good studies, including Niels-Erik Andreasen, *The Christian Use of Time* (Nashville: Abingdon Press, 1978), can be of assistance.

Lay leaders, by drawing on experiences in their own work, can help ministers think constructively about the stewardship of time. How does one balance crisis and planned activity, the needs of others and one's own needs, the activities in church and in the world, and other competing calls for time and energy?

Reason points to the modern measurement of time as both blessing and curse, as Andreasen explains (p. 29):

> Our ability to accurately measure and use time has made our activities so much more efficient. For example, executives or professional people speak of meeting so many half-hour appointments and, if necessary, of sandwiching in a few extra ones by careful timing. This can only be done by people who synchronize their activities down to the minute through a careful and precise management of time. But our use of time in this way also carries a curse, for our ability to measure and use time with great accuracy has given time an unsurpassed tyranny over us. How often have we pitted ourselves against the dispassionately and relentlessly moving arms of our watches—and lost. The clock never stops, but we do frequently and are left behind our schedule by that tiny, triumphant tick of our watch.

Discussion of rest and recreation might also take place in addressing this case. In addition, sorting priorities and learning to say no can be subjects of interest and importance.

## EXPENSE ACCOUNT BLUES

Julio Castillo looked at the ledger and chuckled. Poor Bob had run out of names. There was a phone call to W. Whitman, followed by a visit to the store of Henry D. Thoreau. Farther down the page the name R. Frost appeared.

Though amused and somewhat sympathetic toward the fabrication, Castillo now faced a dilemma indeed. As an auditor of S&B Hardware sales and marketing, he would be accountable in turn for this report by Robert Melcher. Further, Melcher had slipped a bit in other ways, too.

Castillo's job description did not include personal counseling with sales personnel. Why, if Gloria Sanders had gotten this report she simply would have disallowed the $218.61 that seemed fabricated and asked Melcher to justify it. But Castillo knew how hard Melcher had worked in earlier years.

Oops, there was another phone call—to Nat Hawthorne. At least Melcher was literate.

Castillo had moved to Atlanta before he got the job with S&B. It paid about the same as the one he left. Now, however, he had more time with his family and other activities. He served on the governing board of the congregation in which he, Maria, and the children worshiped. He enjoyed particularly working in the area of Christian Education, the committee he chaired.

In those church endeavors, Julio Castillo had come to appreciate more about ethics as well as Bible and theology. He had never considered human decisions cut and dried, right or wrong, even though his work in accounting might push him that way from time to time. Castillo studied in a series with other adults the work of Peter Clecak, among others. He saw one's ethical decisions came from one's worldview. Clecak addressed particularly the ethics of self-denial and of self-fulfillment, but Castillo could see other possibilities as well.

As he looked at Robert Melcher's situation, Castillo agonized. Melcher worked the accounts in the Northeast, where competition used to be most fierce. He had done so for nine years now, though certainly Melcher had expected a promotion to sales manager when Baughman left that post. No, an outsider had been hired. Melcher remained a sales representative.

Of late, Castillo had seen Melcher little. One day as he left the office, he had seen Melcher coming from the bar across the street. Melcher had attended the Controls office party, though obviously he was not in that area of work. Castillo had seen him with a glass actively in hand from the time he arrived until Maria came and Julio had departed for dinner with her. Castillo heard some office talk about Melcher missing a few meetings, and scuttlebutt had it he was drinking a lot. But Melcher's hand was still steady and his writing legible, more than could be said for a couple of other salesmen.

And Castillo knew how hard it was on the road. Melcher himself, in friendlier days two years ago, had told of the loneliness and the boredom of selling hardware and visiting clients time after time. Castillo himself had traveled more than enough in his other job.

Salespeople frequently padded expense accounts. Everyone knew that. It was a good way to compensate for unreimbursed things, like gifts for your children on return or entertainment the company would not allow as expense.

But to make visits and calls to America's literary elite of the nineteenth and twentieth centuries! Castillo might simply refuse those items. Chances were that no one else would read the vouchers. After all, they remained small—a pittance in a $300 million company.

Castillo debated. Should he tell Melcher something? Ask him if the road had gotten to him?

### Discussion Notes

How much is a person obligated to protect an employer? How much does helping a friend matter for Christians? In what ways will Julio Castillo be able to help Robert Melcher anyhow?

This begins as a simple case, but discussion of it can lead to an evaluation of the whole system of expense accounts, to parallel consideration of the tax structure, and to other important subjects. It is important not to concentrate on people who work for corporations, just as in other case discussions you need to keep from focusing just on ministers or on teachers.

You may find particular help in the sections of chapter 3 dealing with virtues and vices. The offerings of Sissela Bok might also be particularly useful here. And you may want to read the work by Peter Clecak that Julio studied, *America's Quest for the Ideal Self: Dissent and Fulfillment in the 60s and 70s* (New York: Oxford University Press, 1983).

The casebook *Full Value*, by Oliver F. Williams and John M.

Houck, has already been mentioned. Their subsequent work, *Judeo-Christian Vision and the Modern Business Corporation* (Notre Dame, Ind.: University of Notre Dame Press, 1982), contains even more explicit help in the area.

# Further Reading

## Chapter 1: What Shall I Do?

Chauncey, George A. *Decisions! Decisions!* Atlanta: John Knox Press, 1972.

Fletcher, Joseph. *Situation Ethics: The New Morality.* Philadelphia: Westminster Press, 1966.

Labacqz, Karen. *Professional Ethics: Power and Paradox.* Nashville: Abingdon Press, 1985.

Ramsey, Paul. *Deeds and Rules in Christian Ethics.* New York: Charles Scribner's Sons, 1967.

## Chapter 2: How Do I Choose?

Gustafson, James M. *The Church as Moral Decision-Maker.* Philadelphia: Pilgrim Press, 1976.

Hauerwas, Stanley. *A Community of Character: Toward a Constructive Christian Ethic.* Notre Dame, Ind.: University of Notre Dame Press, 1981.

———. *The Peaceable Kingdom: A Primer in Christian Ethics.* Notre Dame, Ind.: University of Notre Dame Press, 1983.

Yoder, John H. *The Politics of Jesus.* Grand Rapids: Wm. B. Eerdmans Co., 1972.

## Chapter 3: How Shall I Live?

Bok, Sissela. *Lying: Moral Choice in Public and Private Life.* New York: Pantheon Books, 1978.

McClendon, James W., Jr. *Biography as Theology: How Life Stories Can Remake Today's Theology.* Nashville: Abingdon Press, 1974.

Weeks, Louis and Carolyn, and Robert and Alice Evans. *Casebook for Christian Living.* Atlanta: John Knox Press, 1977.

Williams, Oliver F., and John M. Houck. *Full Value: Cases in Christian Business Ethics.* New York: Harper & Row, 1978.

**Chapter 4: How Shall I Grow?**

Erikson, Erik H. *Identity and the Life Cycle.* New York: International Universities Press, 1959.

Gilligan, Carol. *In a Different Voice: Psychological Theory and Women's Development.* Cambridge: Harvard University Press, 1982.

Kohlberg, Lawrence. *The Philosophy of Moral Development.* New York: Harper & Row, 1981.

Levinson, Daniel J., and others. *The Seasons of a Man's Life.* New York: Alfred A. Knopf, 1978.

Piaget, Jean. *The Moral Judgment of the Child.* New York: Free Press of Glencoe, 1960.

Sheehy, Gail. *Passages: Predictable Crises of Adult Life.* New York: E. P. Dutton Co., 1976.

Printed in the United States
5597